SMALL-GROUP CURRICULUM

# RESPECTABLE SINS

## CONFRONTING THE SINS WE TOLERATE

# JERRY BRIDGES

DISCUSSION GUIDE BY STEPHEN SORENSON

NAVPRESS
Discipleship Inside Out™

**Discipleship Inside Out™**

NavPress is the publishing ministry of The Navigators, an international Christian organization and leader in personal spiritual development. NavPress is committed to helping people grow spiritually and enjoy lives of meaning and hope through personal and group resources that are biblically rooted, culturally relevant, and highly practical.

**For a free catalog go to www.NavPress.com**
**or call 1.800.366.7788 in the United States or 1.800.839.4769 in Canada.**

ISBN-13: 978-1-61521-577-5

Cover design by Arvid Wallen
Cover image by Jupiter Images

Some of the anecdotal illustrations in this book are true to life and are included with the permission of the persons involved. All other illustrations are composites of real situations, and any resemblance to people living or dead is coincidental.

Unless otherwise identified, all Scripture quotations in this publication are taken from the *English Standard Version* (ESV), copyright © 2001 by Crossway Bibles, a division of Good News Publishers. Used by permission. All rights reserved. Other versions used include: the *HOLY BIBLE: NEW INTERNATIONAL VERSION*® (NIV®), Copyright © 1973, 1978, 1984 by International Bible Society, used by permission of Zondervan Publishing House, all rights reserved; *The New Testament in Modern English* (PH), J. B. Phillips Translator, © J. B. Phillips 1958, 1960, 1972, used by permission of Macmillan Publishing Company; *THE MESSAGE* (MSG). Copyright © 1993, 1994, 1995, 1996, 2000, 2001, 2002, 2005. Used by permission of NavPress Publishing Group; and the *King James Version*.

Printed in the United States of America

1 2 3 4 5 6 7 8 / 14 13 12 11 10

# Contents

# Preface

"He that is without sin among you, let him first cast a stone at her" (John 8:7, KJV). Though many scholars today question whether the well-known account of the woman accused of adultery actually belongs in the gospel of John, the expression has become a part of our wider culture, along with a similar one: "Judge not, that ye be not judged" (Matthew 7:1, KJV).

This book, as the title announces, is about sin — not the obvious sins of our culture but the subtle sins of believers, the target audience of this book. So let me say up front that I am not without the sins addressed in this book. In fact, you will find that I sometimes use my own sad experiences as examples of some of these sins.

The motivation for this book stems from a growing conviction that those of us whom I call conservative evangelicals may have become so preoccupied with some of the major sins of society around us that we have lost sight of the need to deal with our own more "refined" or subtle sins.

While seeking to address these "respectable" sins, however, I also want this to be a book of hope. We are never to wallow hopelessly in our sins. Rather, we are to believe the gospel through which God has dealt with both the guilt of our sin and its dominion over us.

The gospel, though, is only for sinners, for those who recognize their need of it. Many Christians think of the gospel as only for unbelievers. Once we trust in Christ, so the thinking goes, we no longer need the gospel. But, as I seek to bring out in this book, the gospel is a vital gift from God not only for our salvation but also to enable us to deal with the ongoing activity of sin in our lives. So we still need the gospel every day.

This book by no means covers all the possible subtle sins we face. A number of friends in Christian ministry looked over a lengthy list of sins I had compiled and helped me reduce it to a manageable list of the more common ones. To those friends I express my deepest thanks for their suggestions.

Three other people deserve special acknowledgment. Don Simpson, who is not only my editor but a close personal friend, has been very helpful. Dr. Bob Bevington, with whom I have just collaborated on another book, also read the manuscript and made helpful suggestions. Mrs. Jessie Newton transferred my handwritten manuscript to a computer composition so that it could be submitted to NavPress. This is the third manuscript Jessie has typed for me. Finally, there are an unknown number of people who have supported this project in prayer. Thanks to all of you for your part in this book.

And above all, to God be the glory both now and forever. Amen.

# Before You Begin

## A NOTE FROM THE AUTHOR

Some years ago a book was published with the title *I'm OK, You're OK*. In contrast to that book title, the attitude of many Christians seems to be "I'm OK and You're Not." That is, we seem to be good at seeing other people's sins but not our own. We see and bemoan the flagrant sins of our culture, and we're even quick to point out the sins of our brothers and sisters in Christ, but we are often blind to the more subtle sins we tolerate in our own lives — those I call "respectable" sins.

You and I may actually be doing quite well when it comes to avoiding the more overt sins. But what about the more subtle ones — the "respectable" sins that can still hinder our walks with God and harm our relationships with others? God has made clear in His Word that He is as dishonored and displeased by our anxiety, unthankfulness, frustration, selfishness, impatience, and discontentment as He is by the overt sins we're so proud to avoid.

In an effort to help us face and deal with these "subtle" sins, I have written *Respectable Sins: Confronting the Sins We Tolerate*. I commend this resource to you as invaluable not only for small-group interaction but also for your own personal study and growth in Christ.

Through experience I have found that we often need more than to merely have our own sins — even the "respectable" ones that we tend to minimize — pointed out to us. We need encouragement and hope, and these come only through the gospel. The good news of Jesus Christ encourages us in our personal struggles with sin because it assures us that in our standing with God, He has already forgiven our sins through the death of His Son on the cross. The gospel gives us hope because it also promises to us the power of the Holy Spirit to enable us to deal with our sins. We need both assurances. We cannot effectively deal with the expressions of our subtle sins until we know they are forgiven. And we cannot effectively deal with our sins apart from the help of the Holy Spirit.

As you use this guide, you will find that I emphasize both of these gospel truths. So do not approach this study with the fear that it will only reveal sin and leave you to wallow in it. Rather, you will find both hope in the gospel and practical suggestions for dealing with your sins. And lest you think that I have written from the perspective of "I'm OK and You're Not," let me assure you that I must deal with many of these sins myself. So together let's confront the subtle sins we tolerate in our lives and implement God's wonderful plan for redemption and victory.

*Jerry Bridges*

## ABOUT THE STUDY

The study questions included in this book serve three important purposes: (1) a road map to enable the group facilitator — the section at the back of the book called "Help for Group Leaders" gives practical suggestions about how to lead a group through this study; (2) a reading and application guide for the group member; and (3) a discussion guide to enhance the group-interaction experience.

You'll be prompted to read specific chapters of the book before each group session. The quality of your personal reading and preparation will help to ensure quality interaction when you get together to discuss what you have read. As you read *Respectable Sins*, keep pen in hand and feel free to underline passages or put stars or question marks in the margins, noting any principles or insights that stand out to you.

After you've read the assigned chapters, you'll respond to the study questions following them. These will help you process some of the key points you've just read. Some questions ask you to look up and respond to selected Bible passages. We strongly encourage you to engage fully with these personal-study opportunities, but if your time is limited and you're able to read only the book chapters before group time, you can come back to the "Think It Through" section later.

At the end of each session you'll find a page titled "Take It to Heart." This page is for you to journal your personal reflections, action points, and prayers in response to the week's reading and discussion. Following the group discussion, find a place of solitude, quiet your heart before God, and then write your responses to the guided Personal Reflection, Personal Action Points, and Personal Prayer prompts we've provided for you. You may find that these journaling exercises are the most meaningful to you of the entire study-and-discussion experience.

We know you're going to enjoy the book and grow in your faith as you sit at the feet of one of the world's most beloved authors and Bible teachers. May God richly bless you, and your group, as you read and discover His blessings together.

*The Editors*

# Facing Up to the Truth

BEFORE GATHERING: Read the following portion of *Respectable Sins*. In the margins, record observations, illustrations, or questions that come to mind as you read. Then answer the "Think It Through" study questions that follow the reading.

---

## Chapter One: Ordinary Saints

Notes and Observations

The church at Corinth was all messed up, both theologically and morally. They were proud and fractious; they tolerated gross immorality, sued each other in court, flaunted their freedom in Christ, abused the observance of the Lord's Supper, misunderstood the purpose of spiritual gifts, and were confused about the future resurrection of believers. Yet when writing to them, Paul addressed them as "saints" (2 Corinthians 1:1) or as those "called to be saints" (1 Corinthians 1:2).

The popular meaning of words often changes over time, based on their common usage. So today we wouldn't think of those messed-up Corinthians as saints. We might call them worldly, carnal, or immature, but certainly not saints. In the Roman Catholic tradition, sainthood is conferred posthumously on Christians of exceptionally outstanding character and achievement. I write these words a few months after the death of the greatly admired Pope John Paul II, and already there is a widespread popular sentiment to canonize him as a saint.

Apparently, over the course of church history, most of the original apostles, including Paul, came to be called saints. My grandfather was a member of St. Paul's Methodist Church. In our city we have St. John's Baptist Church. A Presbyterian friend of mine pastors St. Andrew's Chapel. I have preached in

St. Thomas's Anglican Church. Even Matthias, the apostle chosen to replace Judas, gets into the act with St. Matthias's Church in Sydney, Australia. And, of course, standing above them all in eminence is St. Peter's Basilica in the Vatican.

Today, outside the Roman Catholic and Orthodox traditions, the word *saint* is seldom used. But when it is, it is most often used to describe a person (usually elderly) of unusually godly character. Someone might say, "If there ever was a saint, it is my grandmother." Upon hearing such a statement, we immediately picture a kind, gracious woman who regularly reads her Bible and prays and who is known for her good deeds toward others.

How then could the apostle Paul address the messed-up believers at Corinth as saints? In fact, this form of address seems to be a favorite of Paul's. He uses it in several of his letters and frequently refers to believers as saints (see, for example, Romans 1:7; 16:15; 1 Corinthians 1:2; 2 Corinthians 1:1; Ephesians 1:1; Philippians 1:1; 4:21-22; and Colossians 1:2). How could Paul refer to *ordinary believers*, even the problem-plagued ones at Corinth, as saints?

The answer lies in the meaning of the word as it is used in the Bible. The Greek word for saint is *hagios*, and it refers not to one's character but to a state of being. Its literal meaning is "one who is separated unto God." In this sense, every believer — even the most ordinary and the most immature — is a saint. The actual wording of Paul's address in 1 Corinthians is to "those sanctified in Christ Jesus, called to be saints" (1:2). Here again, we may be surprised with Paul's use of the word *sanctified*, a word we usually associate with holy living. But the words *sanctified* and *saint* both come from the same Greek word family. A saint is simply someone who is sanctified. Although it sounds awkward in English, we could literally rewrite Paul's words as "to those separated in Christ Jesus, called to be separated ones."

Separated for what? A better question is, *Separated for whom?* And the answer is, "for God." Every true believer has been separated or set apart by God for God. Paul, in one place, described our Lord Jesus Christ as the One who gave Himself for us to redeem us from all lawlessness and to purify for Himself a people for His own possession who are zealous for good works (see Titus 2:14). And in 1 Corinthians 6:19-20, Paul says to us, "You are not your own, for you were bought with a price." Together, these two passages help us understand the biblical meaning of saint. It is someone whom Christ bought with His own blood on the cross and has separated unto Himself to be His own possession.

What does it mean to be separated, or set apart? A good analogy is to be found at the U.S. Air Force Academy near our home. Entering first-year cadets are treated vastly different from the way freshman entering public or private universities are treated. From the time they get off the bus at the Academy grounds and throughout their first year, they are subjected to extremely rigorous discipline designed to transform them from easygoing American teenagers into well-disciplined cadets preparing to become military officers. Although this discipline is progressively relaxed as the cadets pass through their four years, it is never completely removed. Even as seniors, they are still subjected to demanding academic and behavioral requirements.

Why is there this difference between the Academy and a typical university? These young men and women have been in a real sense "set apart" by the U.S. government to become Air Force officers. It costs our government over $300,000 to educate and train each cadet over a four-year period. So the Academy doesn't exist to prepare young people to be schoolteachers or Wall Street bankers. It exists for one purpose: to prepare officers for the U.S. Air Force. And the cadets are "set apart" for that purpose.

In a way similar to a young person entering the Air Force Academy, every new believer has been set apart by God, separated unto God to be transformed into the likeness of His Son, Jesus Christ. In this sense, every believer is a saint — a person separated from his old sinful way of life and set apart by God to increasingly glorify God as his life is transformed.

In the biblical sense of the term, sainthood is not a status of achievement and character but a state of being — an entirely new condition of life brought about by the Spirit of God. Paul describes it as "[turning] from darkness to light and from the power of Satan to God" (Acts 26:18) and again as having been "delivered . . . from the domain of darkness and transferred . . . to the kingdom of His beloved Son" (Colossians 1:13).

We don't become saints by our actions. We are made saints by the immediate supernatural action of the Holy Spirit alone who works this change deep within our inner being so that we do, in fact, become new creations in Christ (see 2 Corinthians 5:17). This change of state is described prophetically in Ezekiel 36:26: "I will give you a new heart, and a new spirit I will put within you. And I will remove the heart of stone [a dead, unresponsive heart] from your flesh and give you a heart of flesh [a living, responsive heart]."

It would be nice if we could end the story here, because the last two paragraphs might suggest a saint is someone who no longer sins. Alas, we all know that is not true. Rather, if we are honest with ourselves, we know that nearly every waking hour, we sin in thought, word, or deed. Even our best deeds are stained with impure (mixed) motives and imperfect performance. And who of us can ever begin to say, "I have loved my neighbor as myself"? And of course, the messed-up Corinthian church stands as Exhibit A that we saints can be quite sinful in our attitudes and actions.

Why is this true? Why is there a disconnect between what God has seemingly promised and what we experience in our daily lives? The answer is found in such Scriptures as Galatians 5:17, which says, "The desires of the flesh are against the Spirit, and the desires of the Spirit are against the flesh, for these are opposed to each other, to keep you from doing the things you want to do."

The guerrilla warfare between the flesh and the Spirit described in Galatians 5:17 is fought daily in the heart of every Christian. That is why, for instance, Peter urges us "to abstain from the passions of the flesh, which wage war against your soul" (I Peter 2:11). So although 2 Corinthians 5:17 and Ezekiel 36:26 speak of a decisive change that always occurs in the heart of every new believer, the outworking of that change is not instantaneous and absolute. Instead it is progressive over time and never complete in this life. However, the awareness of this internal struggle with sin should never be used as an excuse for sinful behavior. Rather, we should always keep in mind that we are saints called to live a life that is set apart for God.

So Paul begins his first letter to the Corinthian church by addressing them as "those sanctified [set apart by God] in Christ Jesus, called to be saints [set-apart ones]." Then he spends the remainder of his letter *vigorously exhorting them to act like saints*. In one sense, Paul's letter could be summarized in this statement: "You are saints. Now act like saints!" Sometimes that idea is expressed more succinctly as, "Be what you are." That is, be in your behavior what you are in your state of being. So although the word *saint* basically describes our new state of being as people separated unto God, it carries with it the idea of responsibility to live as saints in our daily lives.

When I was serving as an officer in the U.S. Navy some fifty years ago, there was an expression: "conduct unbecoming an officer." That expression covered anything from minor offenses resulting in a reprimand to major ones requiring a court martial. But the expression was more than a description of aberrant behavior; it was a statement that the conduct was inconsistent with that expected of a military officer. The officer so described had failed to live up to his responsibility to act as an officer should act.

Perhaps we might do well to adopt a similar expression for believers: "conduct unbecoming a saint." Such an expression would pull us up short, wouldn't it? When we gossip or become impatient or get angry, we could remind ourselves that our conduct is unbecoming a saint. We are, in principle, if not in degree, acting like the Corinthians. We are living inconsistently with our calling.

13

The Bible has a word for conduct unbecoming a saint. It is *sin*. And just as "conduct unbecoming an officer" covers a wide range of misconduct, so the word *sin* covers a wide range of misbehavior. It covers everything from gossip to adultery, from impatience to murder. Obviously, there are degrees of seriousness of sin. But in the final analysis, sin is sin. It is conduct unbecoming a saint.

One of our problems, however, is that we neither think of ourselves as saints — with our new state's concurrent responsibility to live as saints — nor do we think of such actions as our gossip and impatience as sin. Sin is what people outside our Christian communities do. We can readily identify sin in the immoral or unethical conduct of people in society at large. But we often fail to see it in what I call the "acceptable sins of the saints." In effect, we, like society at large, live in denial of our sin. So now let's move on to talk about sin and our frequent denial of it in our lives.

---

## Chapter Two: The Disappearance of Sin

In his 1973 book *Whatever Became of Sin?* psychiatrist Karl Menninger wrote,

> The very word, "sin," which seems to have disappeared, was once a proud word. It was once a strong word, an ominous and serious word. . . . But the word went away. It has almost disappeared — the word, along with the notion. Why? Doesn't anyone sin anymore? Doesn't anyone believe in sin?

To reinforce his observations, Dr. Menninger noted that in the presidential proclamation for the annual National Day of

Prayer, the last time the word *sin* was mentioned was in President Eisenhower's proclamation in 1953 — and those words were borrowed from a call to national prayer by Abraham Lincoln in 1863! So, as Dr. Menninger observed, "as a nation, we officially ceased 'sinning' some twenty [now over fifty] years ago."[1]

Karl Menninger is by no means alone in his assessment. Author Peter Barnes, in an article titled "What! Me? A Sinner?" wrote,

> In twentieth century England, C. S. Lewis noted that, "The barrier I have met is the almost total absence from the minds of my audience of any sense of sin." And in 2001, New Testament scholar D. A. Carson commented that the most frustrating aspect of doing evangelism in universities is the fact that students generally have no idea of sin. "They know *how to sin* well enough, but they have no idea of what constitutes sin."[2]

These statements only confirm what seems clear to many observers: The whole idea of sin has virtually disappeared from our culture.

Unfortunately, the idea of sin is all but disappearing from many churches as well. Sociologist Marsha Witten analyzed forty-seven taped sermons on the prodigal son (see Luke 15:11-32) preached by Baptist and Presbyterian ministers. In her book *All Is Forgiven*, she wrote,

> How does the idea of sin fare in the sermons under study here? We should not be surprised to find that communicating notions of sin poses difficulties for many of the pastors. . . . As we have seen here, a closer examination of the sermons suggests the many ways in which the concept of "sin" has been accommodated to fit secular sensibilities. For while some traditional images of sin are retained in this speech, the language

frequently cushions the listeners from their impact, as it employs a variety of softening rhetorical devices.[3]

Ms. Witten concluded her chapter on the pastors' treatment of sin with this observation: "In this context, talk about sin appears more to be setting implicit boundaries to separate insiders who are beyond reach of evaluation from outsiders who are targets for it, than to be articulating theological insights into the depravity of human nature."[4]

So we see that the entire concept of sin has virtually disappeared from our American culture at large and has been softened, even within many of our churches, to accommodate modern sensibilities. Indeed, strong biblical words for sin have been excised from our vocabulary. People no longer commit adultery; instead they have an affair. Corporate executives do not steal; they commit fraud.

But what about our conservative, evangelical churches? Has the idea of sin all but disappeared from us also? No, it has not disappeared, but it has, in many instances, been *deflected* to those outside our circles who commit flagrant sins such as abortion, homosexuality, and murder, or the notorious white-collar crimes of high-level corporate executives. It's easy for us to condemn those obvious sins while virtually ignoring our own sins of gossip, pride, envy, bitterness, and lust, or even our lack of those gracious qualities that Paul calls the fruit of the Spirit (see Galatians 5:22-23).

A pastor invited the men in his church to join him in a prayer meeting. Rather than praying about the spiritual needs of the church as he expected, all of the men without exception prayed about the sins of the culture, primarily abortion and homosexuality. Finally, the pastor, dismayed over the apparent self-righteousness of the men, closed the prayer meeting with the well-known prayer of the tax collector, "God, be merciful to me, a sinner" (Luke 18:13).

The attitude toward sin reflected in the prayers of those

men seems all too prevalent within our conservative, evangelical circles. Of course, this is a broad-brush observation, and there are many happy exceptions. But on the whole, we appear to be more concerned about the sins of society than we are the sins of the saints. In fact, we often indulge in what I call the "respectable" or even "acceptable" sins without any sense of sin. Our gossip or unkind words about a brother or sister in Christ roll easily off our tongues without any awareness of wrongdoing. We harbor hurts over wrongs long past without any effort to forgive as God has forgiven us. We look down our religious noses at "sinners" in society without any sense of a humble "there but for the grace of God go I" spirit.

We were incensed, and rightfully so, when a major denomination ordained a practicing homosexual as a bishop. Why do we not also mourn over our selfishness, our critical spirit, our impatience, and our anger? It's easy to let ourselves off the hook by saying, these sins are not as bad as the flagrant ones of society. But God has not given us the authority to establish values for different sins. Instead, He says through James, "Whoever keeps the whole law but fails in one point has become accountable for [is guilty of] all of it" (2:10). That Scripture is difficult for us to understand because we think in terms of individual laws and their respective penalties. But God's law is seamless. The Bible speaks not of God's *laws*, as if many of them, but of God's *law* as a single whole. When a person commits murder, he breaks God's law. When a Christian lets corrupting speech (that is, speech which tends to tear down another person) come out of his mouth (see Ephesians 4:29), he breaks God's law.

In chapter 1 I acknowledged that some sins are more serious than others. I would rather be guilty of a lustful look than of adultery. Yet Jesus said that with that lustful look, I have actually committed adultery in my heart. I would rather be angry at someone than to murder that person. Yet Jesus said that whoever murders and whoever is angry with his brother are both liable to judgment (see Matthew 5:21-22). The truth is,

17

all sin is serious because all sin is a breaking of God's law.

The apostle John wrote, "Sin is lawlessness" (1 John 3:4). All sin, even sin that seems so minor in our eyes, is lawlessness. It is not just the breaking of a single command; it is a complete disregard for the law of God, a deliberate rejection of His moral will in favor of fulfilling one's own desires. In our human values of civil laws, we draw a huge distinction between an otherwise "law-abiding citizen" who gets an occasional traffic ticket and a person who lives a "lawless" life in contempt and utter disregard for all laws. But the Bible does not seem to make that distinction. Rather, it simply says sin — that is, all sin without distinction — is lawlessness.

In Greek culture, *sin* originally meant to "miss the mark," that is, to miss the center of the target. Therefore sin was considered a miscalculation or failure to achieve. There is some truth in that idea even today as, for example, when a person is genuinely repentant over some sinful behavior and is earnestly seeking to overcome it but still fails frequently. He wants to hit the bull's-eye every time, but he can't seem to pull it off. Usually, however, our sinful actions stem not from a failure to achieve but from an inner urge to fulfill our own desires. As James wrote, "Each person is tempted when he is lured and enticed by his own desire" (1:14). We gossip or lust because of the sinful pleasure we get out of it. At that time, the lure of that momentary pleasure is stronger than our desire to please God.

Sin is sin. Even those sins that I call "the acceptable sins of the saints" — those sins that we tolerate in our lives — are serious in God's eyes. Our religious pride, our critical attitudes, our unkind speech about others, our impatience and anger, even our anxiety (see Philippians 4:6); all of these are serious in the sight of God.

The apostle Paul, in stressing the need to seek justification by faith in Christ alone, quoted from the Old Testament, "Cursed be everyone who does not abide by all things written in the Book of the Law, and do them" (Galatians 3:10). That is a perfectly exacting standard of obedience. In academic terms, that means a 99 on a final exam is a failing grade. It means that a misplaced comma in an otherwise fine term paper would garner an F. Now, happily, Paul goes on to assure us that Christ has "redeemed us [that is, all who trust in Him as their redeemer] from the curse of the law by becoming a curse for us" (Galatians 3:13). But the fact still remains that the seemingly minor sins we tolerate in our lives do indeed deserve the curse of God.

Yes, the whole idea of sin may have disappeared from our culture. It may have been softened in many of our churches so as not to make the audiences uncomfortable. And, sad to say, the concept of sin among many conservative Christians has been essentially *redefined* to cover only the obviously gross sins of our society. The result, then, is that for many morally upright believers, the awareness of personal sin has effectively disappeared from their consciences. But it has not disappeared from the sight of God. Rather, all sin, both the so-called respectable sins of the saints, which we too often tolerate, and the flagrant sins of society, which we are quick to condemn, are a disregard for the law of God and are reprehensible in His sight. Both deserve the curse of God.

If this observation seems too harsh and too sweeping an indictment of believers, let me hasten to say that there are many godly, humble people who are happy exceptions. In fact, the paradox is that those whose lives most reflect the fruit of the Spirit are usually those who are most keenly aware of and groan inwardly over these so-called acceptable sins in their own lives. But there is also a vast multitude who are quite judgmental toward the grosser sins of society but who seem pridefully unaware of their own personal sins. And a lot of us live somewhere in between. But the point is, all of our sin, wherever we may be on the spectrum of personal awareness of it in our lives, is reprehensible in the sight of God and deserving of His judgment.

Admittedly, I have painted a rather dark picture, both of

Notes and Observations

society as a whole and of our conservative, evangelical community. But God has not forsaken us. For those who are true believers, God is still our heavenly Father, and He is at work among us to call us to repentance and renewal. Part of His calling is to lead us to the place where we do see the sins we tolerate in our own lives so that we will experience the repentance and renewal we need. It is my prayer that God will be pleased to use this book as one means to that end. And so for one more chapter, we will dig deeper into the sinfulness of our "respectable" sins.

## Chapter Three: The Malignancy of Sin

Cancer! It's a dreaded word, a word that often invokes a sense of despair and sometimes even hopelessness. For me, cancer was always something that happened in other families. But in 1987, it came to our family when my wife was diagnosed with non-Hodgkin's lymphoma. I remember my reaction: This can't be happening to us. But it had, and seventeen months later, my wife died after a debilitating and even humiliating illness.

Another term for cancer is malignancy. Medically, the word *malignant* describes a tumor of potentially unlimited growth that expands locally into adjoining tissue by invasion and systemically by metastasizing into other areas of the body. Left alone, a malignancy tends to infiltrate and metastasize throughout the entire body and will eventually cause death. No wonder *cancer* and *malignant* are such dreaded words.

Sin is a spiritual and moral malignancy. Left unchecked, it can spread throughout our entire inner being and contaminate every area of our lives. Even worse, it often will "metastasize" from us into the lives of other believers around us. None of us lives on a spiritual or social island. Our attitudes, words, and actions, and oftentimes even our private unspoken thoughts, tend to have an effect on those around us.

Paul must have had this concept in mind when he wrote, "Let no corrupting talk come out of your mouths, but only such as is good for building up, as fits the occasion, that it may give grace to those who hear" (Ephesians 4:29). Our speech, whether it is about others or to others, tends to tear down or build up. It either corrupts the minds of our hearers, or it gives grace to them. Such is the power of our words. If I gossip, I both tear down another person and corrupt the mind of my listener. If I complain about the difficult circumstances of my life, I impugn the sovereignty and goodness of God and tempt my listener to do the same. In this way, my sin "metastasizes" into the heart of another person.

Sin, however, is much more than wrong actions, unkind words, or even those evil thoughts that we never express. Sin is a principle or moral force in our heart, our inner being. Our sinful actions, words, and thoughts are simply expressions of the principle of sin residing within us, even in those of us whose hearts have been renewed. The apostle Paul calls this principle the *flesh* (or *sinful nature* in some Bible translations). This principle, called the flesh, is such a reality that Paul sometimes personifies it (see, for example, Romans 7:8-11; Galatians 5:17).

Now, here is the unvarnished truth that we need to lay to heart. Even though our hearts have been renewed, even though we have been freed from the absolute dominion of sin, even though God's Holy Spirit dwells within our bodies, this principle of sin still lurks within us and wages war against our souls. It is the failure to recognize the awful reality of this truth that provides the fertile soil in which our "respectable" or "acceptable" sins grow and flourish.

We who are believers tend to evaluate our character and conduct relative to the moral culture in which we live. Since we usually live at a higher moral standard than society at large, it is easy for us to feel good about ourselves and to assume that God feels that way also. We fail to reckon with the reality of sin still dwelling within us.

One of the common truths about cancer is that it can often grow undetected until it reaches a crisis stage or even a stage that is terminal. When my wife visited her doctor on June 19, 1987, she had no idea there was a malignant tumor growing in her abdominal area. And even her capable physicians who successfully treated the tumor failed to detect that it had already metastasized into her lymph system. In fact, the word *deceitful*, which is a moral term, can be used to describe the way cancer often seems to operate. It seems to have been successfully treated; but unexpectedly, it reappears somewhere else in the body.

The way cancer operates is a good analogy of the way sin, especially so-called acceptable or refined sin, operates in our lives. As I mentioned in the preface, another good descriptive term is *subtle sins*. The word *subtle* has a wide variety of meanings, some positive, as in "the subtle shades of blue in a painting." But often it has a strong negative connotation to mean wily, crafty, insidious, or treacherous. That is the sense of the word in the expression *subtle sins*. The acceptable sins are subtle in the sense that they deceive us into thinking they are not so bad, or not thinking of them as sins, or even worse, not even thinking about them at all! Yes, some of our refined sins are so subtle that we commit them without even thinking about them, either at the time or afterward. We often live in unconscious denial of our "acceptable" sins.

We present-day believers have, to some extent, been influenced by the "feel good about myself" philosophy of our times. By contrast, believers in the Puritan era of the seventeenth century had a different view of themselves. They feared the reality of sin still dwelling in them. I have in my library four books on sin by pastors of that era. Here are their titles:

*The Sinfulness of Sin*

*The Mischief of Sin*

*The Anatomy of Secret Sins*

*The Evil of Evils or The Exceeding Sinfulness of Sin*

These pastors all saw sin for what it actually is: a diabolical force within us. Ralph Venning, the author of *The Sinfulness of Sin*, uses especially colorful (in the negative sense) words to describe sin. Over the space of only a few pages, he says that sin is vile, ugly, odious, malignant, pestilent, pernicious, hideous, spiteful, poisonous, virulent, villainous, abominable, and deadly.

Take a few moments to ponder those words so as to get the full impact of them. Those words describe not just the scandalous sins of society but also the respectable sins we tolerate in our own lives. Think of such tolerated sins as impatience, pride, resentment, frustration, and self-pity. Do they seem odious and pernicious to you? They really are. To tolerate those sins in our spiritual lives is as dangerous as to tolerate cancer in our bodies. Seemingly small sins can lead to more serious ones. Lustful looks often lead to pornography addiction and perhaps even adultery. Murder often has its genesis in anger, which grows into bitterness, then to hatred, and finally the murder.

About this time, you may be tempted to throw this book across the room. You didn't pick it up to be condemned or to have your subtle sins exposed. So far everything in this book seems dark and dismal. You want to be encouraged, not condemned. If you feel that way, I appeal to you to stay with me. We are indeed going to get to some good news later on. But for now, we've got to continue to explore the bad news. In fact, it is going to get worse. When we see how really bad the bad news is, we'll be in a better position to appreciate how really good the good news is.

So how does the already bad news get worse? So far we've looked at our sin as it affects us. We've seen its malignant tendency in both our lives and the lives of others around us. The more important issue, however, is how our sin affects God. Someone has described sin as cosmic treason. If that seems like an overstatement, consider that the word *transgression* in the Bible, as seen for example in Leviticus 16:21, actually means rebellion against authority — in this case, God's authority. So when I gossip, I am rebelling against God. When I harbor resentful thoughts toward someone instead of forgiving him or her in my heart, I am rebelling against God.

In Isaiah 6:1-8, the prophet Isaiah sees a vision of God in His absolute majesty. He hears angelic beings calling out, "Holy, holy, holy is the LORD of hosts; the whole earth is full of his glory!" (verse 3). Any Jew would have understood that the threefold repetition of the word *holy* is intended to convey the highest possible degree of holiness. In other words, God is said to be infinitely holy. But what does it mean to say that God is infinitely holy? Certainly it speaks of His absolute moral purity, but it means much more than that. Primarily, the word *holy*, when used of God, speaks of His infinite, transcendent majesty. It speaks of His sovereign reign over all His creation. Therefore, when we sin, when we violate the law of God in any way, be it ever so small in our eyes, we rebel against the sovereign authority and transcendent majesty of God. To put it bluntly, our sin is an assault on the majesty and sovereign rule of God. It is indeed cosmic treason.

Let's continue with the bad news. Remember the story of David's sin of adultery with Bathsheba and then his arranging the death of her husband, Uriah, to try to cover up his adultery? God was displeased, to put it mildly, and sent Nathan the prophet to confront David about his sin. Here are Nathan's words:

> Why have you *despised* the word of the LORD, to do what is evil in his sight? You have struck down Uriah the Hittite with the sword and have taken his wife to be your wife and have killed him with the sword of the Ammonites. Now therefore the sword shall never depart from your house, because you have *despised* me and have taken the wife of Uriah the Hittite to be your wife. (2 Samuel 12:9-10, emphasis added)

Note the use of the word *despised* in both verses 9 and 10. In the first instance David despises the word (the law) of the Lord. In the second instance, God, speaking through Nathan, says, "You have despised me." We see from this that sin is a despising of the law of God. But we also see that to despise God's law is to despise Him. Now, it is easy for us to think that David's sin truly was grievous and fail to grasp the application of Nathan's words to ourselves. But as we have already seen, all sin, whether large or small in our eyes, is against God. Therefore, when I indulge in any of the so-called acceptable sins, I am not only despising God's law but, at the same time, I am despising God Himself. Think about that the next time you are tempted to speak critical or unkind words about someone. Do you see why I said that our description of sin would get worse?

We're not through yet. There's still more bad news. In the context of exposing sin in our relationships with one another (see Ephesians 4:25-32), Paul says, "Do not grieve the Holy Spirit of God, by whom you were sealed for the day of redemption" (verse 30). When we think of our sin as rebellion against God's sovereign authority and a despising of both His law and His person, we are viewing God in His rightful role as our ruler and judge. But when we see our sin as grieving the Holy Spirit — that is, as grieving God — we are viewing God as our redeemer and Father. Our sin grieves our heavenly Father. Whether we are unkind to someone else or unforgiving when someone is unkind to us, we grieve our Father's heart.

Not only do we grieve our heavenly Father with our sin, we also presume on His grace. Paul wrote that God has forgiven us our trespasses, according to the riches of His grace (see Ephesians 1:7). Now, that is a blessed truth, but sin, in its subtle deceitfulness, will suggest to us that our unkind words and resentful thoughts don't matter because God has forgiven them. Forgiveness, however, does not mean overlooking or tolerating our sin. God never does that. Instead, God *always* judges sin. But in our case (that is, the case of all who trust in Jesus

25

as their Savior), God has judged our sin in the person of His Son. As the prophet Isaiah wrote, "All we like sheep have gone astray; we have turned every one to his own way; and the LORD has laid on him the iniquity of us all" (Isaiah 53:6). Shall we presume on God's grace by tolerating in ourselves the very sin that nailed Christ to the cross?

Next consider that every sinful thought and word and deed we do is done in the presence of God. David wrote,

> O LORD, you have searched me and known me!
> You know when I sit down and when I rise up;
>     you discern my thoughts from afar.
> You search out my path and my lying down
>     and are acquainted with all my ways.
> Even before a word is on my tongue,
>     behold, O LORD, you know it altogether.
>     (Psalm 139:1-4)

God knows our every thought; He hears our words before we even speak them and sees our every deed. He even searches our motives, for Paul wrote that when the Lord comes, He "will disclose the purposes [motives] of the heart" (1 Corinthians 4:5).

This means that all of our rebellion, all of our despising of God and His law, all of our grieving His Holy Spirit, all of our presuming on His grace, all of our sin, is done openly in the very presence of God. It's as if we are acting out all of our sin before Him as He sits on His royal throne.

I referred earlier to the Puritan Ralph Venning's book *The Sinfulness of Sin*. The title sounds somewhat like a tautology, a needless repetition. But in his title, Venning was trying to make a point, and here is his point in his own words: "On the contrary, as God is holy, all holy, only holy, altogether holy, and always holy, so sin is sinful, all sinful, only sinful, altogether sinful, and always sinful.[5] It does not matter whether our sin is scandalous or respectable, all our sin is sinful, only sinful, and altogether sinful. Whether it is large or small in our eyes, it is heinous in the sight of God. God forgives our sin because of the shed blood of Christ, but He does not tolerate it. Instead, every sin that we commit, even the subtle sin that we don't even think about, was laid upon Christ as He bore the curse of God in our place. And herein lies chiefly the malignancy of sin. Christ suffered because of our sins.

That, then, is the bad news about our sin, and, as you can see, it is really, really bad. How do you respond? Will you deflect it onto other people whom you see to be sinners? Do you find yourself wishing that a certain other person would read this chapter? Or does this view of our sin cause you to want to fall on your knees before God in repentance and contrition over the sins you have tolerated in your life? If the latter is true, then you are ready for the good news, and it really is really, really good.

# Facing Up to the Truth

## (Chapters 1, 2, and 3)

## STUDY QUESTIONS

KEY VERSE: "Sin is lawlessness." (1 John 3:4)

### GET FOCUSED

Some forms of cancer grow undetected until they reach a terminal stage. Likewise, sin — especially the so-called "acceptable" or "subtle" sins — can exist in our lives, virtually undetected and dangerous. We can be deceived into believing that such sin is not all that bad, into denying that sin is really sin, and into not thinking about sin. In fact, the word *sin* has virtually disappeared from our culture — and is even avoided in some churches. Well-intentioned believers find it all too easy to focus on the blatant sins of our "evil" culture while ignoring their own, more-subtle sins — "respectable" sins.

In contrast to the feel-good-about-ourselves philosophy of our day, Puritan believers in the seventeenth century had a different view of themselves and sin. They feared the reality of sin; they saw all sin as a diabolical force living within themselves. They recognized, like the biblical writers, that *any* sin breaks God's law.

During this session we will explore the impact of sins that Christians tend to downplay in their own lives — sins such as impatience, gossip, pride, resentment, and anger. These often become larger malignancies, cascading us into deeper sinfulness.

Yes, God sent Jesus to earth to take humankind's sins on Himself. But as long as we believers recognize our call to glorify God and become like Jesus, we will battle sin. To live as God's people includes facing sin — especially sin we don't recognize or we rationalize away. That's what this first session is all about.

THINK IT THROUGH
FOR PERSONAL STUDY

### I. *What Is Sin?*

1. Why do you think it's important for us to understand what sin is and its impact on our lives and relationships?

2. What do James 1:14-15 and 2:10-11 reveal about the root of our sinful actions? About God's law and the consequences of breaking it?

3. In Matthew 5:22,27-28, what did Jesus emphasize concerning the seriousness of sin — of breaking God's law?

### II. *What Happened to the Word Sin?*

1. What evidence do you see that the word *sin* has virtually disappeared from our culture? That awareness of personal sin has effectively disappeared from many believers' consciences? Explain your answer.

**What's Become of Sin?**

The very word, *sin*, which seems to have disappeared, was once a proud word. It was once a strong word, an ominous and serious word. . . . But the word went away. It has almost disappeared — the word, along with the notion. Why? Doesn't anyone sin anymore? Doesn't anyone believe in sin?

KARL MENNINGER
*Whatever Became of Sin?* [6]

2. What impact do you think the "softening" of language regarding sin is having on our lives? On our churches?

3. Why is it often easier for believers to focus on the sins of unbelievers rather than on their own personal sins?

### III. "Respectable" Sins

1. List some common "respectable" sins. Why do you think we are more inclined to tolerate them?

2. In Galatians 3:10, what did the apostle Paul quote to emphasize the importance of obeying God's law? What might this reveal about the consequences of tolerating "seemingly minor sins"?

3. Even though God always makes a decisive change in every believer's heart, what does every believer face when he or she seeks to live in obedience to God? (See Galatians 5:17; James 1:14.)

4. Describe the choices Peter and Paul urge every true believer to make. (See Galatians 5:16; Ephesians 4:29; 1 Peter 2:11.)

### IV. How Our Sin Affects God

1. Jerry writes: "When we sin we violate the law of God in any way, . . . we rebel against the sovereign authority and transcendent majesty of God. We commit 'cosmic treason.'" It is indeed "cosmic treason." Do you agree or disagree with the concept of "cosmic treason"? Explain.

2. How much do you think God knows about our sin? (See Psalm 139:1-4; 1 Corinthians 4:5.)

3. Read 2 Samuel 12:1-10, where Nathan the prophet spoke God's words to David, who had committed adultery with Bathsheba, murdered her husband, and lived in denial of his sin. What do we learn about denial? About sin in relation to God and His law?

4. What effect does sin have on the Holy Spirit — that is, God — who lives inside each believer? (See Ephesians 4:30.)

## TALK IT OVER
### FOR GROUP DISCUSSION

1. Why should we take our "respectable" sins seriously?

2. How might we begin to see our own sins more clearly instead of focusing so much on other people's sins?

3. What impact do you think the "softening" of language regarding sin is having on our lives? On our churches?

4. As we realize that our sin is not only rebellion against God's sovereign authority but a despising of both His law and His person, how might we view sin differently?

5. How might what we learned today influence what we say, do, and/or think?

## GROUP PRAYER

As a group, thank God for the opportunity to gather and explore this important topic. Ask Him to help you recognize "respectable" sins and to take them seriously.

❧ ❧

FOR NEXT TIME: Read *Respectable Sins*, chapters 4, 5, and 6, then respond to the "Think It Through" personal-study questions for session 2.

---

## TAKE IT TO HEART
### *A PERSONAL-GROWTH JOURNAL*

### *Personal Reflection*

During this session, what discoveries, quotations, or verses especially connected with you? Why?

What "respectable" sins might you be tolerating in your life?

In what ways might these sins be affecting your life, your relationships, and your relationship with God?

What do you think God wants you to learn from that situation?

### *Personal Action Point*

What one insight regarding "respectable" sins would you like to begin applying to your spiritual journey this week? Write it down and commit it to the Lord.

### *Personal Prayer*

Write a brief prayer to God about sin's lure and impact in your life — and your desire for Him to help you stand strong in the face of temptation.

## PROGRESS REPORT

What have you discovered this week about "respectable" sins?

As you have begun to apply what you learned from session 1, what new choices have you made? What challenges have you faced?

In what ways has knowing God's view of all sin — including the more "acceptable" ones — influenced you this week?

# The Remedy for Sin

BEFORE GATHERING: Read the following portion of *Respectable Sins*. In the margins, record observations, illustrations, or questions that come to mind as you read. Then answer the "Think It Through" study questions that follow the reading.

---

### Chapter Four: The Remedy for Sin

Notes and Observations

John Newton, who wrote the much-loved hymn "Amazing Grace," was earlier in his life a slave trader and even captain of a ship transporting captured Africans to America. For medical reasons, he left the seafaring life, became a customs officer, studied theology, and eventually became a minister. However, even as a minister, Newton never forgot the horrible nature of his sin as a slave trader. At the end of his life, Newton said to a friend, "My memory is nearly gone; but I remember two things: that I am a great sinner, and that Christ is a great Savior."[1]

Centuries before, Saul of Tarsus, who became the apostle Paul, was also guilty of grievous sins. Acts 7:54–8:1 describes his complicity in the stoning of Stephen; then in Acts 9:1-2, we read of his personal involvement in persecuting believers. Toward the end of his life, Paul described himself in those earlier days as "a blasphemer, persecutor, and insolent opponent [of Christ]" (1 Timothy 1:13). But in that same context, he could also say, "Christ Jesus came into the world to save sinners, of whom I am the foremost" (1 Timothy 1:15).

Both John Newton and the apostle Paul saw themselves as great sinners, but with a great Savior. Most believers cannot identify with either John Newton or the apostle Paul in the gravity of their earlier sins. We may not have committed adultery,

35

murdered anyone, dealt drugs, or embezzled from our employers. I myself, reflecting back on my life, can say I was usually an obedient child, a model teenager, a trusted employee, and a conscientious husband and father. In fact, I've even been on the staff of a Christian ministry for over fifty years.

However, though I have not committed any of the big scandalous sins, I have gossiped, spoken critically of others, harbored resentment, become impatient, acted selfishly, failed to trust God in difficult issues of life, succumbed to materialism, and even let my favorite football team become an idol. I have to say with Paul that I am the foremost of sinners. Or to paraphrase John Newton's words, "I am a great sinner, but I have a great Savior." That is my only hope. That is the only remedy for my sin, and it is your only remedy as well.

Both John Newton and Paul spoke of themselves as sinners in the present tense. Neither of them said I *was*; they said I *am*. It's clear in the context of Paul's statement that he was reflecting on his earlier sins as a persecutor. Likewise, we know from Newton's own reflections that he never got over the fact that he had been a slave trader. In fact, with each passing year, he became more horrified at his former life.

Does that mean, then, that though describing themselves as sinners in the present tense, they were referring only to their past sins as a persecutor and a slave trader? It is hardly possible that they would think that way. We know, for instance, that several years before writing 1 Timothy, Paul referred to himself as "the very least of all the saints" and as a minister of the gospel only by the grace of God (see Ephesians 3:7-8). In fact, there seems to be a downward progression in Paul's self-awareness from the least of the apostles (see 1 Corinthians 15:9, written in AD 55) to the very least of all the saints (see Ephesians 3:8, written in AD 60) to the foremost of sinners (see 1 Timothy 1:15, written about AD 63 or 64).

We can be sure that over the years from their conversion to their death, both Newton and Paul grew in Christlike character. Over time, both of them acted more and more as the saints they had become at conversion. But that growth process involved becoming more aware of and sensitive to the sinful expressions of the flesh still dwelling within them. And so John Newton could have easily said, "I *was* and *still am* a great sinner, but I have a great Savior." And if you and I are to make any progress in dealing with the acceptable sins of our lives, we must say the same.

The remedy for our sin, whether scandalous or acceptable, is the gospel in its widest scope. The gospel is actually a message; here I am using the word *gospel* as a shorthand expression for the entire work of Christ in His historic life, death, and resurrection for us, and His present work in us through His Holy Spirit. When I say the gospel in its widest scope, I am referring to the fact that Christ, in His work for us and in us, saves us not only from the penalty of sin but also from its dominion or reigning power in our lives. This twofold aspect of Christ's great work is beautifully captured in Augustus Toplady's great hymn "Rock of Ages," with the words,

> Let the water and the blood,
> From thy riven side which flowed,
> Be of sin the double cure,
> Cleanse me from its guilt and power.[2]

Beginning with session 3, we will be getting specific about many of the respectable sins in our lives — what they look like, the damage they cause, and how to deal with them. But before we do that, we need to take a good look at the gospel. We need to do this for several reasons.

First, the gospel is only for sinners. Christ Jesus came into the world to save sinners (see 1 Timothy 1:15). Most Christians tend to think of the gospel as applicable only to unbelievers who need to be "saved." Once we trust in Christ, so the thinking goes, the gospel doesn't apply to us anymore, except to share it with others who are still unbelievers. However, though we truly are saints in the sense of being separated unto God, all of us are still practicing sinners. All the ethical commands and exhortations addressed to believers in the New Testament assume there is still sin present in our lives that needs to be addressed. Among the four uses for which Scripture is profitable, as described in 2 Timothy 3:16, are reproof and correction. Again, these uses assume that we still have sin that needs to be reproved and corrected.

So the first use of the gospel, as a remedy for our sins, is to plow the ground of our hearts so that we can see our sin. Stepping forward to accept my place as a sinner in need of the gospel each day drives a dagger into my self-righteous heart and prepares me to face up to and accept the reality of the sin that still dwells within me.

Second, not only does the gospel prepare me to face my sin, it also frees me up to do so. Facing our sin causes us to feel guilty. Of course we *feel* guilty because we *are* guilty. And if I believe, consciously or unconsciously, that God still counts my guilt against me, my instinctive sense of self-protection forbids me to acknowledge my sin and guilt, or, at the least, I seek to minimize it. But we cannot begin to deal with a particular manifestation of sin, such as anger or self-pity, until we first openly acknowledge its presence and activity in our lives. So I need the assurance that my sin is forgiven before I can even acknowledge it, let alone begin to deal with it.

By acknowledging my sin, I mean more than a halfhearted admission to myself that I acted selfishly in a given instance. Rather, I mean a wholehearted, defenseless admission, "I am a selfish person, and that particular act was only a manifestation of the selfishness that still dwells within me." But in order to make such an admission, I need the assurance that my selfishness is forgiven — that God no longer holds it against me. The gospel gives us that assurance. Consider these words from the apostle Paul: "Blessed are those whose lawless deeds are forgiven, and whose sins are covered; blessed is the man against whom the Lord will not count his sin" (Romans 4:7-8).

Why does God not count my sins against me? Because He has already charged it to Christ. As the prophet Isaiah wrote, "All we like sheep have gone astray; we have turned every one to his own way; and the LORD has laid on him the iniquity of us all" (53:6).

To the extent that I grasp, in the depth of my being, this great truth of God's forgiveness of my sin through Christ, I will be freed up to honestly and humbly face the particular manifestations of sin in my life. That's why it is so helpful to affirm each day with John Newton that "I am a great sinner, but I have a great Savior."

Third, the gospel motivates and energizes me to deal with my sin. It is not enough to honestly face our sin. If we are to grow in Christlike character, we must also deal with it. To use a scriptural term, we must "put it to death" (see Romans 8:13; Colossians 3:5). But as has been well said, the only sin that can be successfully fought against is forgiven sin. We cannot begin to deal with the *activity* of sin in our lives until we have first dealt with its guilt. So here again we go back to the gospel and its assurance that God through Christ has dealt with our guilt.

The assurance that God no longer counts my sin against me does two things. First it assures me that God is for me, not against me (see Romans 8:31). I am not alone in this battle with sin. God is not watching me from His heavenly throne saying, "When are you going to get your act together? When are you going to deal with that sin?" Rather, He is, as it were, coming alongside me saying, "We are going to work on that sin, but meanwhile I want you to know that I no longer count it against you." God is no longer my Judge; He is now my heavenly Father, who loves me with a self-generated, infinite love, even in the face of my sin. That assurance greatly encourages me and motivates me to deal with the sin.

Further, the assurance that God no longer counts my sin against me, and that in my struggles with sin, He is for me, produces within me a strong sense of gratitude for what He has

39

done and is presently doing for me through Christ.

This twofold effect of encouragement and gratitude together produce in us a *desire* to deal with our sin. Make no mistake: Dealing with our sin is not an option. We are commanded to put sin to death. It is our duty to do so. *But duty without desire soon produces drudgery.* And it is the truth of the gospel, reaffirmed in our hearts daily, that puts desire into our duty. It is the gospel that stokes the fire of our motivation to deal with our respectable and subtle sins. It is the gospel that motivates us to seek to be in our daily experience what we are in our standing before God.

We can see, then, that the continuous day-by-day appropriation of the gospel, as it assures us of the forgiveness of our sins, is an important part of our dealing with sin in our lives. It is not the only part — and we will consider some others in later sessions — but for now, I urge you to commit yourself to a daily, conscious appropriation of the gospel.

Some years ago, I heard a man use the expression, "Preach the gospel to yourself every day." That is what we must do in order to daily, consciously appropriate the gospel. We must preach it to ourselves every day. Not only that, we need to personalize it to ourselves, as Paul did when he wrote of "the Son of God, who loved *me* and gave himself for *me*" (Galatians 2:20, emphasis added). It is also helpful to personalize the Father's love in a similar manner. For example, we can paraphrase 1 John 4:10 to say, "In this is love, not that [*I*] have loved God but that he loved [*me*] and sent his Son to be the propitiation [to bear the wrath of God] for [*my*] sins" (emphasis added).

The good news that God no longer counts my sin against me, that He has in fact forgiven me of all my sin, is so radical, so contrary to our normal way of thinking that, frankly, it seems too good to be true. Especially on a day when circumstances have made you vividly aware of your selfishness, impatience, or resentment, it does seem too good to be true. Even while writing this chapter, I had such a day, and I had to go to the

40

Scriptures, actually read the assurances of God's forgiveness from the pages of the Bible, and "preach" them to myself. But it doesn't matter if we're having a "bad" day or a "good" day. Even on what seems like our very best days, we still need to preach the gospel to ourselves. The truth is, there is never a day in our lives when we are so "good" we don't need the gospel.

At this point, you may be wondering, *If preaching the gospel to myself is so important, how do I do it?* There is no set way, so I will share my practice only as an illustration. I am by nature a methodical person, so my way will not suit everyone, but hopefully it will give any reader some idea of what preaching the gospel looks like in one person's life. So here is my way.

Since the gospel is only for sinners, I begin each day with the realization that despite my being a saint, I still sin every day in thought, word, deed, and motive. If I am aware of any subtle, or not so subtle, sins in my life, I acknowledge those to God. Even if my conscience is not indicting me for conscious sins, I still acknowledge to God that I have not even come close to loving Him with all my being or loving my neighbor as myself. I repent of those sins, and then I apply specific Scriptures that assure me of God's forgiveness to those sins I have just confessed.

I then generalize the Scripture's promises of God's forgiveness to all my life and say to God words to the effect that my only hope of a right standing with Him that day is Jesus' blood shed for my sins, and His righteous life lived on my behalf. This reliance on the twofold work of Christ for me is beautifully captured by Edward Mote in his hymn "The Solid Rock" with his words, "My hope is built on nothing less, than Jesus' blood and righteousness." Almost every day, I find myself going to those words in addition to reflecting on the promises of forgiveness in the Bible.

What Scriptures do I use to preach the gospel to myself? Here are just a few I choose from each day:

41

As far as the east is from the west, so far does he remove our transgressions from us. (Psalm 103:12)

"I, I am he who blots out your transgressions for my own sake, and I will not remember your sins." (Isaiah 43:25)

All we like sheep have gone astray; we have turned every one to his own way; and the LORD has laid on him the iniquity of us all. (Isaiah 53:6)

Blessed are those whose lawless deeds are forgiven, and whose sins are covered; blessed is the man against whom the Lord will not count his sin. (Romans 4:7-8)

There is therefore now no condemnation for those who are in Christ Jesus. (Romans 8:1)

There are many others, including Psalm 130:3-4; Isaiah 1:18; Isaiah 38:17; Micah 7:19; Ephesians 1:7; Colossians 2:13-14; Hebrews 8:12; and 10:17-18.[3]

Whatever Scriptures we use to assure us of God's forgiveness, we must realize that whether the passage explicitly states it or not, the *only* basis for God's forgiveness is the blood of Christ shed on the cross for us. As the writer of Hebrews said, "without the shedding of blood there is no forgiveness of sins" (9:22), and the context makes it clear that it is Christ's blood that provides the objective basis on which God forgives our sins.

This, then, is the first part of the good news of the gospel; God has forgiven us all our sins through the death of His Son on the cross. To refer back to Toplady's hymn "Rock of Ages," this is the first part of the "double cure" — that is, being cleansed of sin's guilt. But Toplady's "double cure" also included being cleansed from sin's power, and that is the subject of our next chapter.

## Chapter Five: The Power of the Holy Spirit

Augustus Toplady's hymn speaks of the "double cure" — that is, cleansing from both sin's guilt and power. In the previous chapter, we saw that God does indeed cleanse us from sin's guilt through the death of His Son. God does not forgive because He wants to be lenient with us. He forgives because His justice has been satisfied. The absolute forgiveness of our sins is just as rock solid as the historic reality of Christ's death. It is important that we grasp this wonderful truth of the gospel because we can face our "respectable" sins only when we know they are forgiven.

However, Toplady's hymn speaks not only of cleansing from sin's guilt but also from its power. Sometimes when we are struggling with some particular expression of our sin, we wonder if the gospel does address the power of sin in our lives. We wonder if we will ever see progress in putting to death some persistent sin pattern that we struggle with. Can we honestly say with Toplady that Christ, the "Rock of Ages," does indeed cleanse us from sin's power as well as its guilt?

To answer that question, we need to see the cleansing from sin's power in two stages. The first is deliverance from the dominion or reigning power of sin that is decisive and complete for all believers. The second is freedom from the remaining presence and activity of sin that is progressive and continues throughout our lives on earth. Paul helps us see this twofold deliverance in Romans 6.

In Romans 6:2, Paul writes that we "died to sin," and in verse 8, he says, "We have died with Christ." That is, through our union with Christ in His death, we have died, not only to sin's guilt but also to its reigning power in our lives. This is true

43

of every believer and is accomplished at the time of our salvation when God delivers us from the domain of darkness and transfers us to the kingdom of His Son (see Colossians 1:13).

Paul's statement that "we died to sin" is a declarative statement. It is something God has done for us at the moment of our salvation. Nothing we do subsequent to that decisive transaction can add to or subtract from the fact that we died to both sin's guilt and dominion.

At the same time, however, Paul urges us to "let not sin therefore reign in your mortal bodies, to make you obey their passions" (Romans 6:12). How can sin possibly reign if we have died to it? Here Paul is referring to the continued presence and ceaseless activity of sin that, though it is "dethroned" as the reigning power over our lives, still seeks to exert a controlling influence in our daily walk. It, so to speak, continues to wage a spiritual guerrilla warfare in our hearts. This warfare is described by Paul in Galatians 5:17:

> The desires of the flesh are against the Spirit, and the desires of the Spirit are against the flesh, for these are opposed to each other, to keep you from doing the things you want to do.

We experience this struggle between the desires of the flesh and the desires of the Spirit daily. This tension causes us to sometimes wonder if the gospel really does address this aspect of sin's power — that is, its ability to pull us toward its desires. This seems especially true in the more respectable sins in our lives. Some of these subtle sins seem tenacious, and we must battle them daily. With others, we sometimes think we've turned the corner on one, only to discover a few days later that we've only gone around the block and are dealing with it again.

At this point in our struggle, we are prone to think, *It's fine to be told sin no longer has dominion over me, but what about my daily experience of the remaining presence and activity of sin? Does the gospel cleanse me from that? Can I hope to see progress in putting to death the subtle sins of my life?*

Paul's answer to that pressing question is found in Galatians 5:16: "I say, walk by the Spirit, and you will not gratify the desires of the flesh." To walk by the Spirit is to live under the controlling influence of the Spirit and in dependence upon Him. Paul says that as we do this, we will not gratify the desires of the flesh.

Practically speaking, we live under the controlling influence of the Spirit as we continually expose our minds to and seek to obey the Spirit's moral will for us as revealed in Scripture. We live in dependence on Him through prayer as we continually cry out to Him for His power to enable us to obey His will.

There is a fundamental principle of the Christian life that I call the principle of *dependent responsibility*; that is, we are responsible before God to obey His Word, to put to death the sins in our lives, both the so-called acceptable sins and the obviously not acceptable ones. At the same time, we do not have the ability within ourselves to carry out this responsibility. We are in fact totally dependent upon the enabling power of the Holy Spirit. In this sense, we are both responsible and dependent.

As we seek to walk by the Spirit, we will, over time, see the Spirit working in us and through us to cleanse us from the remaining power of sin in our lives. We will never reach perfection in this life, but we will see progress. It will be incremental progress, to be sure, and sometimes it will appear to be no progress at all. But if we sincerely want to address the subtle sins in our lives, we may be sure the Holy Spirit is at work in us and through us to help us. And we have His promise that "he who began a good work in you will bring it to completion at the day of Jesus Christ" (Philippians 1:6). The Holy Spirit will not abandon the work He has begun in us.

Actually, as we carefully read the New Testament letters, we see that the writers, especially Paul, ascribe this work in us sometimes to God the Father, then to Jesus the Son, and at other times to the Holy Spirit. The truth is, all three members of the divine Trinity are involved in our spiritual transformation, but the Father and the Son work through the Holy Spirit who dwells in us (see 1 Corinthians 6:19). For example, Paul prays to the Father that we will be strengthened with power *through His Spirit* in our inner being (see Ephesians 3:16). And as someone has said so well, "The Spirit conveys what Christ bestows." So when I speak of the power of the Holy Spirit, I am speaking of the power of the Father, Son, and Holy Spirit that is communicated to us and worked out in us by the Holy Spirit.

How the Holy Spirit works in us and through us is a mystery in the sense that we cannot comprehend or explain it. We simply accept the testimony of Scripture that He dwells in us and is at work in us to transform us more and more into the likeness of Christ (see 2 Corinthians 3:18). We do need to actively believe this great truth about the Holy Spirit. We need to believe that, as we seek to deal with our subtle sins, we are not alone. He is at work in us, and we will see progress as we walk by the Spirit.

One of the ways the Holy Spirit works in us is to bring conviction of sin. That is, He causes us to begin to see our selfishness, our impatience, or our judgmental attitude as the sins that they truly are. He works through the Scriptures (which He inspired) to reprove and correct us (see 2 Timothy 3:16). He also works through our consciences as they are enlightened and sensitized by exposure to His Word. I have even known Him to bring to my memory a specific act of a subtle sin and, using that single act as a starting point, begin to point out to me a pattern of that sin in my life. It stands to reason that conviction of sin must be one of His vital works because we cannot begin to deal with a sin, especially one that is common and acceptable in our Christian culture, until we have first realized that the particular pattern of thought, word, or deed is indeed sin.

Another way in which the Holy Spirit works in us is to enable and empower us to deal with our sin. In Romans 8:13, Paul exhorts us *by the Spirit* to "put to death the deeds of the body." In Philippians 2:12-13, he urges us to "work out [our] own salvation . . . for it is God who works in you, both to will and to work for his good pleasure." That is, Paul urges us to work in the confidence that God is at work in us. Though Paul refers to *God*, presumably God the Father, as the One at work, we have already seen that God works through the Holy Spirit as the transforming agent in our lives.

Then we read in Philippians 4:13 Paul's words that "I can do all things through him who strengthens me." We can deal with our pride, our impatience, our critical and judgmental spirit as we depend on the Holy Spirit to empower and enable us. Thus, we should never give up. Regardless of how little progress we seem to make, He is at work in us. Sometimes He seems to withhold His power, but this may be to cause us to learn experientially that we truly are dependent on Him.

In addition to His empowering work to enable us to work, the Holy Spirit also works in us monergistically; that is, He works alone without our conscious involvement. In His benediction in Hebrews 13:20-21, the writer speaks of God "working in us that which is pleasing in his sight." That particular truth should greatly encourage us. Even in our most dismal days when we see little progress in the battle with sin, we can be confident the Holy Spirit is still at work in us. It is quite possible that though He is grieved by our sin (see Ephesians 4:30), He may even use that sin to humble us and to exercise us to cry out to Him with a sense of greater dependency.

Still another way in which the Holy Spirit works for our transformation is by bringing into our lives circumstances that are designed to cause us to grow spiritually. Just as our physical muscles will not grow in strength without exercise, so our spiritual life will not grow apart from circumstances that challenge us.

If we are prone to sinful anger, there will be circumstances that trigger our anger. If we tend to be judgmental toward others, we will probably have plenty of occasions to be judgmental. If we easily become anxious, there will be ample opportunities to deal with the sin of anxiety. God does not tempt us to sin (see James

47

1:13-14), but He does bring or allow circumstances to come into our lives that give us opportunity to put to death the particular subtle sins that are characteristic of our individual lives. It is obvious that we can deal with the activity of our subtle sins only as the circumstances we encounter expose them.

Of course, all I have written in the last two paragraphs assumes that God is absolutely in sovereign control of all our circumstances. There are numerous passages of Scripture that affirm this, but one that states this truth most explicitly is Lamentations 3:37-38: "Who has spoken and it came to pass, unless the Lord has commanded it? Is it not from the mouth of the Most High that good and bad come?"

There are many applications that we can draw from this passage, but the truth I want us to see now is that God is in control of every circumstance and every event of our lives, and He uses them, often in some mysterious way, to change us more into the likeness of Christ.

Romans 8:28 is a text many of us go to for encouragement in tough times. For those who do not recognize the reference, it says, "We know that for those who love God all things work together for good, for those who are called according to his purpose." However, while that passage is indeed one of all-around encouragement to us, Paul is actually talking about our spiritual transformation. The "good" of verse 28 is explained in verse 29 to be conformity to the image of God's Son. This means, then, that the Holy Spirit is at work in us through our circumstances to make us more like Christ.

So in summary we see that the Holy Spirit works in us to convict us and make us aware of our subtle sins. He then works in us to enable us to put to death those sins. Then He works in us in ways of which we are not conscious. And then He uses the circumstances of our lives to exercise us in the activity of dealing with our sins.

We do have a vital part to play. We are responsible to put to death the acceptable sins in our lives. We cannot simply lay this responsibility on God and sit back and watch Him work. At the same time, we are dependent. We cannot make one inch of spiritual progress apart from His enabling power.

But the Holy Spirit does more than help us. He is the one actually directing our spiritual transformation. He uses means, of course, and I pray that He will use even this book to help us all uncover and deal with the subtle sins in our lives. But He does not leave us to our own insight to see our sins or our own power to deal with them.

So Augustus Toplady's words are true: God does deliver us from both sin's guilt and power through the atoning death of Christ on the cross and the mysterious but very real work of the Holy Spirit in our lives.

Therefore, as we move into the section of this book where we begin to look at our acceptable sins in detail, take heart. Remember, Christ has already paid the penalty for our sins and won for us the forgiveness of them. And then He has sent His Holy Spirit to live within us to enable us to deal with them.

I also urge you to pray that the Holy Spirit will enable you to see the hidden, subtle sins in your life. Sin is deceitful (see Ephesians 4:22). It will cause you to live in complete denial of a particular sin or mitigate the seriousness of it. Only the Holy Spirit can successfully expose a sin for what it is.

Be prepared to be humbled. I well remember the occasion when the Holy Spirit revealed to me selfishness in my life. Up to that time, I had always defined selfishness in terms of the obvious, overt selfishness I saw in the lives of a few other people. It was humbling to admit I was also selfish, but in a much more subtle way. Jesus, however, promised blessing to those who are poor in spirit — that is, to those who face up to their sins and mourn because of them. He also promised blessing to those who hunger and thirst for righteousness — that is, to those who earnestly desire to see the sin in their lives put to death and replaced with the positive fruit of the Spirit (see Matthew 5:4,6; Galatians 5:22-23).

49

## Chapter Six: Directions for Dealing with Sins

We have looked at the remedy for sin and the power of the Holy Spirit working in our favor. We've also seen that we must play an active role in dealing with sin. The apostle Paul wrote that we are to "put to death" the various expressions of sin in our lives (see Romans 8:13; Colossians 3:5). This includes not only obvious sins we want to avoid but also the more subtle ones we tend to ignore. It's not enough to agree that we do tolerate at least some of them. Anyone except for the most self-righteous person will acknowledge that. "After all, no one is perfect," may be our attitude. But to honestly face those sins is another matter. For one thing, it is quite humbling. It also implies that we must do something about them. We can no longer continue to ignore them as we have in the past.

Before addressing some of the specific areas of acceptable sins among Christians, however, I want to give some directions for dealing with them. While there may be particular helps for certain ones, there are general directions that apply to all our subtle sins.

The *first* direction is that we should always address our sin in the context of the gospel. I have covered this truth already in chapter 4, but it needs repeating at this point. Our tendency is that as soon as we begin to work on an area of sin in our lives, we forget the gospel. We forget that God has already forgiven us our sin because of the death of Christ. As Paul wrote in Colossians 2:13-14, "[God has] forgiven us all our trespasses, by canceling the record of debt that stood against us with its legal demands. This he set aside, nailing it to the cross."

Not only has God forgiven us our sins, He has also credited to us the perfect righteousness of Christ. In every area of life where we have been disobedient, Jesus was perfectly obedient. Are we prone to be anxious? Jesus always perfectly trusted His heavenly Father. Do we have trouble with selfishness? Jesus was always completely self-giving. Are we guilty of unkind words, gossip, or sarcasm? Jesus spoke only those words that would be appropriate for each occasion. He never once sinned with His tongue.

For some thirty-three years, Jesus lived a life of perfect obedience to the moral will of God, and then He culminated that obedience by being obedient to the Father's specific will for Him — an obedience unto death, even death on the cross for our sins. In both His sinless life and His sin-bearing death, Jesus was perfectly obedient, perfectly righteous, and it is that righteousness that is credited to all who believe (see Romans 3:21-22; Philippians 3:9).

As we struggle to put to death our subtle sins, we must always keep in mind this twofold truth: Our sins are forgiven and we are accepted as righteous by God because of both the sinless life and sin-bearing death of our Lord Jesus Christ. There is no greater motivation for dealing with sin in our lives than the realization of these two glorious truths of the gospel.

The *second* direction is that we must learn to rely on the enabling power of the Holy Spirit. Remember, it is by the Spirit that we put to death the sins in our lives (see Romans 8:13). Again, we have already addressed this truth in detail in chapter 5, but as with the gospel, we tend to forget it and resort to our own willpower. It's what I call one of our "default settings." Regardless of how much we grow, however, we never get beyond our constant need of the enabling power of the Holy Spirit. Our spiritual life may be compared to the motor of an electric appliance. The motor does the actual work, but it is constantly dependent upon the external power source of the electricity to enable it to work. Therefore, we should cultivate an attitude of continual dependence on the Holy Spirit.

The *third* direction is that, while depending on the Holy Spirit, we must at the same time recognize our responsibility to diligently pursue all practical steps for dealing with our sins. I know that keeping both these truths — that is, our dependence and our responsibility — equally in mind is difficult. Our tendency is to emphasize one to the neglect of the other. Here the wisdom of some of the older writers will help us: "Work as if it all depends on you, and yet trust as if you did not work at all."

The *fourth* direction is that we must identify specific areas of acceptable sins. That is one of the purposes of the following sessions as we take up many of the subtle sins one by one. As you read each chapter, ask the Holy Spirit to help you see if there is a pattern of that sin in your life. This, of course, requires a humble attitude and a willingness to face that sin. As you identify a particular sin, give thought to what situations trigger it. Anticipating the circumstances or events that stimulate the sin can help in putting it to death.

The *fifth* direction is that we should bring to bear specific applicable Scriptures to each of our subtle sins. These Scriptures should be memorized, reflected on, and prayed over as we ask God to use them to enable us to deal with those sins. The psalmist wrote, "I have stored up your word in my heart, that I might not sin against you" (119:11). To *store up* means to lay aside for future need.

In 1999, there was a tremendous wave of anxiety around the world as to what might happen when all the world's computer clocks turned over to January 1, 2000. There were all kinds of dire predictions that the world's commerce, which is now so heavily dependent on computers, would simply shut down. As a result, many people stored up extra food and emergency items. This event, known as Y2K, turned out to be a nonevent, as the computers did not shut down. Nevertheless, that occasion powerfully illustrates the meaning of the phrase *stored up*. People were storing up against a time of future need.

That is what we do when we commit Scripture texts to our hearts. We store them up against future needs: the times when we are tempted to indulge our subtle (or even our not so subtle) sins.

Of course, memorizing specific Scripture verses is no magic bullet. They must be applied to our lives. But if we have memorized and prayed over Scriptures that address our subtle sins, the Holy Spirit will bring them to mind in particular situations to remind us of the will of God, to warn us, and to guide us in our response to the temptation. To help you in this, I will recommend certain Scriptures that might be helpful as we take up the individual acceptable sins.

The *sixth* direction is that we should cultivate the practice of prayer over the sins we tolerate. This is assumed in the second direction about relying on the Holy Spirit and in the fifth direction regarding praying over the Scriptures we memorize. But it is important to single out prayer as one of our major directions for dealing with sin, for it is through prayer that we consciously acknowledge our need of the Holy Spirit, and it is through prayer that we continually acknowledge the presence of those persistent sin patterns in our lives.

Prayers regarding our subtle sins should be of two types. First, we should pray over them in a planned, consistent manner, probably in our daily private time with God. Second, we should pray short, spontaneous prayers for the help of the Holy Spirit each time we encounter situations that might trigger one of our sins.

The *seventh* direction is that we should involve one or more other believers with us in our struggles against our subtle sins. This, of course, should be a mutual relationship as we seek to exhort, encourage, and pray for one another. The Scripture tells us that "two are better than one, because they have a good reward for their toil. For if they fall, one will lift up his fellow. But woe to him who is alone when he falls and has not another to lift him up!" (Ecclesiastes 4:9-10). We need the mutual vulnerability with and accountability to one another, as well as the praying for one another and encouraging one another, if we want to make progress in dealing with sin.

Do all these directions seem overwhelming? If so, perhaps this summary will help:

53

- Apply the gospel.
- Depend on the Holy Spirit.
- Recognize your responsibility.
- Identify specific respectable sins.
- Memorize and apply appropriate Scriptures.
- Cultivate the practice of prayer.
- Involve one or a few other believers with you.

As you seek to apply these directions, remember that your heart is a battleground between the flesh and the Spirit (see Galatians 5:17). In this guerrilla warfare, the flesh will sometimes get the upper hand. And as you zero in on a particular sin to seek to put it to death, your situation may get worse before it gets better. Take heart: This is not unusual. The Holy Spirit will use these times of disobedience and defeat to help you see how deeply rooted your subtle sins are and how totally dependent you are on His power to help you.

Now as we turn to examine specific sins that we often tolerate, I will usually offer other practical suggestions that are appropriate to those sins. But the seven general directions will always apply, so I suggest you thoroughly digest this chapter before moving on.

# The Remedy for Sin

## (Chapters 4, 5, and 6)

## STUDY QUESTIONS

KEY VERSES: "Blessed are those whose lawless deeds are forgiven, and whose sins are covered; blessed is the man against whom the Lord will not count his sin." (Romans 4:7-8)

## GET FOCUSED

The apostle Paul and John Newton (writer of the hymn "Amazing Grace") viewed themselves as great sinners who had a great Savior — Jesus Christ.

Before meeting Jesus, Saul (renamed Paul) persecuted believers (See Acts 7:54–8:3). Toward the end of his life, Paul described himself as "the very least of all the saints" (Ephesians 3:8) and a "blasphemer, persecutor, and insolent opponent [of Christ]" (1 Timothy 1:13). He also wrote, "Christ Jesus came into the world to save sinners, of whom I am the foremost" (1 Timothy 1:15).

John, a former slave trader and slave-ship captain, never forgot his slave-related sin but focused on Jesus. "My memory is nearly gone," John said at the end of his life, "but I remember . . . that I am a great sinner, and that Christ is a great Savior."[4]

As Paul and John grew Christlike, they became increasingly aware of, and sensitive to, their sin. They described themselves as sinners in the present tense — "I *am*," not "I *was*." "And," Jerry Bridges writes, "if you and I are to make any progress in dealing with the acceptable sins of our lives, we must say the same."

Perhaps you find it difficult to identify with the grievous sins Saul and John committed. But have you gossiped, harbored resentment, acted selfishly, or distrusted God? Sin is sin.

The only remedy for our sin lies in the forgiveness of sin Jesus can provide. "The good news that God no longer counts my sin against me," writes the author, ". . . seems too good to be true." But it's not! And the Holy Spirit helps us deal with our sin, directing our spiritual transformation.

## THINK IT THROUGH
### FOR PERSONAL STUDY

### *I. As Followers of Christ, We're Delivered from Sin's Power*

1. The moment we receive salvation through Christ, what does God do for us regarding the guilt and reigning power of sin? (See Romans 6:1-2; Colossians 1:13-14.)

2. What does God use to convict us of our sins — including our selfishness and judgmental attitudes? (See 2 Timothy 3:16.)

### He Won't Let Us Down

If we claim that we're free of sin, we're only fooling ourselves. . . . On the other hand, if we admit our sins — make a clean breast of them — he [God] won't let us down; he'll be true to himself. He'll forgive our sins and purge us of all wrongdoing.

1 John 1:8-9, MSG

3. What assurance do we have that, when we acknowledge our sinfulness and ask for God's forgiveness, He will forgive us and no longer hold our sin against us? (See Romans 4:7-8; Ephesians 1:7; 1 John 1:9.)

4. In Matthew 5:6, what did Jesus promise all who pursue righteousness, who earnestly desire to see their sin put to death and be replaced with the fruit of the Spirit? (See Matthew 5:4,6; Galatians 5:22-23.)

## II. *God Helps Every Believer Deal with Sin*

1. Read Galatians 5:16. What hope is promised as we seek to "put to death" sins that keep coming back? What does it mean to "walk by the Spirit"?

2. As we ask God to enable us to deal with our sin, what must we "store up" in our hearts? (See Psalm 119:11.)

3. How can we be sure that God the Father and the Son, working through the Holy Spirit who lives within every believer (see 1 Corinthians 6:19), will help us deal with sin and direct our spiritual transformation? (See Romans 8:31; Philippians 1:6; 2:12-13.)

4. What is the Holy Spirit doing within each believer? (See 2 Corinthians 3:18.)

TALK IT OVER
FOR GROUP DISCUSSION

1. How does the truth that God has forgiven our sin free us to honestly and humbly face our sin?

2. What hinders us from recognizing our sin? Why do we allow sin to "reign" in our lives? (See Romans 6:12.)

3. How might our lives change if we consistently pray about subtle sins and ask for the Holy Spirit's help each time we encounter situations that might trigger these sins?

4. Why do we, in the author's words, "need to preach the gospel to ourselves," to read biblical assurances of God's forgiveness?

5. How should Jesus' work — the forgiveness that His death and resurrection accomplished — motivate us to deal with our sin?

## GROUP PRAYER

Together, invite God to give each of you a heart that longs to be in intimate relationship with Him — and to promptly confess your sins as His Spirit makes you aware of them.

❧ ❧

FOR NEXT TIME: Read *Respectable Sins*, chapters 7 and 8, and then respond to the "Think It Through" questions for session 3.

---

### TAKE IT TO HEART
*A PERSONAL-GROWTH JOURNAL*

#### *Personal Reflection*

During this session, which insight(s) did you particularly appreciate and why?

If you trust Jesus Christ as your Savior and Lord, do you find it easy or difficult to comprehend God's forgiveness and infinite love for you? Why?

If you're a follower of Christ, God has completely forgiven your sin and will work with you to put to death expressions of sin in your life—including "respectable" ones. What does this mean to you personally?

### Personal Action Point

In this space, write out 1 John 1:9 from your favorite translation of the Bible. Between now and the next session, memorize and reflect on this verse's personal promise.

### Personal Prayer

Write out a brief prayer thanking God for the promise of 1 John 1:9 and what it means to you personally.

---

## PROGRESS REPORT

Share a few ways in which you are becoming more aware of "respectable" sins and how to face them.

Have you tried asking for the Holy Spirit's help when you encounter a situation that might trigger these sins? If so, what happened? If not, why not?

How would you describe the assurance you have that when you contritely confess your sin, God forgives you — no matter what sin you have committed? How is this assurance freeing you to honestly (and often) face up to your sin?

# Ungodliness and Unthankfulness

BEFORE GATHERING: Read the following portion of *Respectable Sins*. In the margins, record observations, illustrations, or questions that come to mind as you read. Then answer the "Think It Through" study questions that follow the reading.

---

## Chapter Seven: Ungodliness

Notes and Observations

When I talk about specific areas of acceptable sins, one comment I often hear is that pride is the root cause of all of them. While I agree that pride does play a major role in the development and expression of our subtle sins, I believe there is another sin that is even more basic, more widespread, and more apt to be the root cause of our other sins. That is the sin of *ungodliness*, of which we are all guilty to some degree.

Does that statement surprise you, or maybe even offend you? We don't think of ourselves as ungodly. After all, we *are* Christians; we are not atheists or wicked people. We attend church, avoid scandalous sins, and lead respectable lives. In our minds, the ungodly folks are the ones who live truly wicked lives. How, then, can I say that we believers are all, to some extent, ungodly?

Contrary to what we normally think, ungodliness and wickedness are not the same. A person may be a nice, respectable citizen and still be an ungodly person. The apostle Paul wrote in Romans 1:18, "The wrath of God is revealed from heaven against all ungodliness and unrighteousness." Note that Paul distinguishes ungodliness from unrighteousness. Ungodliness describes an attitude toward God, while unrighteousness refers to sinful actions in thought, word, or deed. An atheist

Notes and Observations

or avowed secularist is obviously an ungodly person, but so are a lot of morally decent people, even if they say they believe in God.

Ungodliness may be defined as living one's everyday life with little or no thought of God, or of God's will, or of God's glory, or of one's dependence on God. You can readily see, then, that someone can lead a respectable life and still be ungodly in the sense that God is essentially irrelevant in his or her life. We rub shoulders with such people every day in the course of our ordinary activities. They may be friendly, courteous, and help-ful to other people, but God is not at all in their thoughts. They may even attend church for an hour or so each week but then live the remainder of the week as if God doesn't exist. They are not wicked people, but they are ungodly.

Now, the sad fact is that many of us who are believers tend to live our daily lives with little or no thought of God. We may even read our Bibles and pray for a few minutes at the begin-ning of each day, but then we go out into the day's activities and basically live as though God doesn't exist. We seldom think of our dependence on God or our responsibility to Him. We might go for hours with no thought of God at all. In that sense, we are hardly different from our nice, decent, but unbelieving neighbor. God is not at all in his thoughts and is seldom in ours.

One cannot carefully read the New Testament without recognizing how far short we come in living out a biblical stan-dard of godliness. I referred above to our seldom thinking of our dependence on God. In that regard, consider these words from James:

> Come now, you who say, "Today or tomorrow we will go into such and such a town and spend a year there and trade and make a profit" — yet you do not know what tomorrow will bring. What is your life? For you are a mist that appears for a little time and then vanishes.

Instead you ought to say, "If the Lord wills, we will live and do this or that." (4:13-15)

James does not condemn these people for making plans or even planning to set up a business and make a profit. What he condemns is their planning that does not acknowledge their dependence on God. We make plans all the time. In fact, we couldn't live or accomplish the most mundane duties of life without some degree of planning. But so often we act like the people James addressed. We, too, make our plans without recognizing our utter dependence on God to carry them out. That is one expression of ungodliness.

In the same way, we seldom think of our accountability to God and our responsibility to live according to His moral will as revealed to us in Scripture. It's not that we are living obviously sinful lives; it's just that we seldom think about the will of God and, for the most part, are content to avoid obvious sins. Yet Paul wrote to the Colossian believers,

We have not ceased to pray for you, asking that you may be filled with the knowledge of his will in all spiritual wisdom and understanding, so as to walk in a manner worthy of the Lord, fully pleasing to him, bearing fruit in every good work and increasing in the knowledge of God. (1:9-10)

Notice how God-centered that prayer is. Paul wanted his hearers to be full of the knowledge of God's will — that is, His moral will. He desired that they live lives worthy of God and fully pleasing to Him, and he prays to that end. That is God-centered praying. Paul wanted the Colossians to be godly people.

Remember, the Colossian believers were not super-Christians; they were ordinary folks like you and me, living ordinary lives in the midst of an ungodly culture far worse than ours today. Yet Paul expected them to live, and prayed that they would live, godly lives.

How does Paul's prayer for the Colossians compare with our prayers for ourselves, our families, and our friends? Do our prayers reflect a concern for God's will and God's glory and a desire that our lives will be pleasing to God? Or are our prayers more of a do-list we present to God, asking Him to intervene in the various health and financial needs of family and friends. Now, it is not wrong to bring these temporal needs to God. In fact, that's one way we can acknowledge our daily dependence on Him. But if that's all we pray about, we are merely treating God as a "divine bellhop." Our prayers are essentially human-centered, not God-centered, and in that sense we are ungodly to some degree.

For Paul, all of life is to be lived out in the presence of God with an eye to pleasing Him. For example, note how he instructed the slaves in the Colossian church (very likely a large part of the congregation) as to how to serve their masters in a godly fashion:

> Slaves, obey in everything those who are your earthly masters, not by way of eye-service, as people-pleasers, but with sincerity of heart, fearing the Lord. Whatever you do, work heartily, as for the Lord and not for men, knowing that from the Lord you will receive the inheritance as your reward. You are serving the Lord Christ. (3:22-24)

His admonition to "work heartily, as for the Lord and not for men" (verse 23) provides us a principle by which we are to seek to live godly lives in the context of our vocations or professions. Yet how many believers seek to live by this principle in their daily lives? Do we not rather approach our vocations much like our unbelieving and ungodly coworkers who work purely for themselves, their promotions, and their pay raises, with no thought of pleasing God?

Notes and Observations

Or consider the Corinthian church, which, as we have already noted, was so messed up. Yet Paul wrote to them, "So, whether you eat or drink, or whatever you do, do all to the glory of God" (1 Corinthians 10:31). The *all* of that sentence includes every activity of our days. We are not only to eat to the glory of God, we are to drive to the glory of God, we are to shop to the glory of God, and we are to engage in our social relationships to the glory of God. Everything we do is to be done to the glory of God. That is the mark of a godly person.

What, then, does it mean to do all to the glory of God? It means that I eat and drive and shop and engage in my social relationships with a twofold goal. First, I desire that all that I do be pleasing to God. I want God to be pleased with the way I go about the ordinary activities of my day. So I pray prospectively over the day before me, asking that the Holy Spirit will so direct my thoughts, words, and actions that they will be pleasing to God.

Second, to do all to the glory of God means that I desire that all my activities of an ordinary day will honor God before other people. Jesus said, "In the same way, let your light shine before others, so that they may see your good works and give glory to your Father who is in heaven" (Matthew 5:16). By contrast, Paul wrote to the self-righteous Jews in Rome, "You who boast in the law dishonor God by breaking the law. For, as it is written, 'The name of God is blasphemed among the Gentiles because of you'" (Romans 2:23-24). Think of it this way: If everyone you interact with in the course of an ordinary day knows that you trust in Christ as Savior and Lord, would your words and actions glorify God before them? Or would you perhaps be like the father of whom one of his children said, "If God is like my father, I want nothing to do with God"?

Hopefully not many of us would be like the father whose harsh treatment of his children blasphemed God. But how far do we go in a positive direction to seek to glorify God before others? Do we consciously and prayerfully seek His glory in all we say and do in our most ordinary activities of the day? Or do we actually go about those activities with little or no thought of God?

An even more telling indicator of our tendency toward ungodliness is our meager desire to develop an intimate relationship with God. The psalmist wrote, "As a deer pants for flowing streams, so pants my soul for you, O God. My soul thirsts for God, for the living God. When shall I come and appear before God?" (42:1-2).

This is not an isolated text. In Psalm 63:1, David speaks of thirsting for God and earnestly seeking Him. In Psalm 27:4, he wants to dwell in the presence of the Lord so as to gaze upon His beauty. These are the desires of godly men of old. Yet few of us claim those desires as our own today. A person may be moral and upright, or even busy in Christian service, yet have little or no desire to develop an intimate relationship with God. This is a mark of ungodliness.

For the godly person, God is the center and focal point of his or her life. Every circumstance and every activity of life, whether in the temporal or spiritual realms, is viewed through the lens of this God-centeredness. However, such a God-centeredness can be developed only in the context of an ever-growing intimate relationship with God. No one can genuinely desire to please God or glorify Him apart from such a relationship.

If you have followed my reasoning this far, you can see that no Christian is totally godly, and to the extent we are not, there is still some degree of ungodliness in us. The question we should honestly and humbly ask is, *How ungodly am I?* How much of my life do I live without any regard for God? How much of my daily activities do I go through without any reference to God?

Total godliness and utter ungodliness are the opposite ends of a continuum. All of us are somewhere between those two extremes. The only person who ever lived a totally godly life was Jesus. And probably no true believer lives a totally ungodly life. But where are we on the spectrum? As you think about your own life, remember that we are not talking about righteous versus wicked behavior. We are talking about living all of life as if God is relevant or irrelevant. Survey after survey continues to inform us that there is little difference between the values and behavior patterns of Christians and non-Christians. Why is this true? Surely it reflects the fact that we live so much of our ordinary lives with little or no thought of God, or of how we might please and glorify Him. It's not that we consciously or deliberately put God out of our minds. We just ignore Him. He is seldom in our thoughts.

I stated at the beginning of this chapter that I believe ungodliness is our most basic sin, even more basic than pride. Think how it would curb our pride, for example, if we consciously lived every day in the awareness that all we are, all we have, and all we accomplish is by the grace of God. My wife and I were lamenting over two otherwise nice, decent people who are living openly immoral lives and relishing it. And then I reminded my wife and myself that "there but for the grace of God go we." Self-righteous pride, one of the more common of our acceptable sins, is a direct product of our ungodly thinking.

Sins of the tongue, such as gossip, sarcasm, and other unkind words to or about another person, cannot thrive in an awareness that God hears every word we speak. The reason we do sin with our tongues is due to the fact that we are to some degree ungodly. We don't think of living every moment of our lives in the presence of an all-seeing, all-hearing God.

I believe that all our other acceptable sins can ultimately be traced to this root sin of ungodliness. To use a tree as an illustration, we can think of all our sins, big and small, growing out of the trunk of pride. But that which sustains the life of the tree is the root system, in this case the root of ungodliness. It is ungodliness that ultimately gives life to our more visible sins.

If ungodly habits of thinking, then, are so commonplace

with us, how can we deal with this sin? How can we become more godly in our daily lives? Paul wrote to Timothy, "Train yourself for godliness" (1 Timothy 4:7). The word *train* comes from the athletic culture of that day and refers to the practice athletes went through daily to prepare themselves to compete in their athletic contests. It implies, among other things, commitment, consistency, and discipline in training.

Paul wanted Timothy, and all believers of every age, to be just as committed to growth in godliness, and just as intentional in pursuing it, as the athletes of that day who were competing for a temporal prize. But I suspect that most Christians seldom, if ever, think about how they can grow in godliness.

I could not help but contrast our anemic desire for godliness with the attitude of young men in our city who recently camped out all night in snow and cold at the entrance to a local electronics store. They wanted to be sure they would be able to buy one of a limited supply of a new video game system. One young man arrived at 9:30 Saturday morning to wait for the doors to open at 8 a.m. Sunday. Would any of us have that kind of zeal for godliness?

Our goal in the pursuit of godliness should be to grow more in our conscious awareness that every moment of our lives is lived in the presence of God; that we are responsible to Him and dependent on Him. This goal would include a growing desire to please Him and glorify Him in the most ordinary activities of life.

Of course, growth in godliness has to begin with the recognition that we need to grow in that most fundamental area of life. I hope I have made the case that all of us are to some degree ungodly, as we live our daily lives with little or no conscious regard for God. Again let me emphasize that you may be living a morally upright life and be a regular attendee at church but still be ungodly if God is seldom in your thoughts.

I realize mere words on a printed page will not convince anyone that he or she is guilty, to some degree, of ungodliness.

Notes and Observations

For one thing, living one's daily life without regard to God probably doesn't seem like sin to many people. I can ask only that you prayerfully consider the message of this chapter and honestly ask yourself how much of your life is lived with little or no thought of God. What would you do differently in your various activities of the day if you were seeking to do all to the glory of God?

Because ungodliness is so all-encompassing, it will help to identify specific areas of life where you tend to live without regard to God. These might include your work, your hobbies, your playing or watching sports, and even your driving. Scripture texts that might be helpful to memorize, ponder, and pray over include 1 Timothy 4:7-8; 1 Corinthians 10:31; Colossians 1:9-10 and 3:23; as well as Psalm 42:1-2; 63:1; and 27:4.

Above all, pray that God will make you more conscious of the fact that you live every moment of every day under His all-seeing eye. While you may not be mindful of Him, He is certainly aware of you and sees every deed you do, hears every word you say, and knows every thought you think (see Psalm 139:1-4). Beyond that, He even searches out your motives. Let us then seek to be as mindful of Him as He is of us.

## Chapter Eight: Unthankfulness

In Bible times, leprosy was a loathsome disease that ostracized its victims from family and friends. In fact, the Mosaic Law required that anyone with leprosy must continually cry out, "Unclean, unclean," as he walked along the road, lest any passerby be contaminated by his disease (see Leviticus 13:45).

Luke records that Jesus was once met by ten lepers who stood at a distance and cried out to Him, "Jesus, Master, have mercy on us." Jesus said to them, "Go and show yourselves to the priests" (who were the ones who could officially pronounce a leper cleansed from his disease), and as they went they were cleansed. Of the ten cleansed, one, a Samaritan, when he saw that he was healed, returned to Jesus, praising God and thanking Jesus. Jesus then exclaimed, "Were not ten cleansed? Where are the nine? Was no one found to return and give praise to God except for this foreigner?" (see Luke 17:11-19).

We read this story and we think, "How could those nine men be so ungrateful as to not even turn back and say a word of thanks to Jesus?" And yet far too many of us are guilty of the same sin of unthankfulness.

Spiritually, our condition was once far worse than the physical disease of leprosy. We were not diseased; we were spiritually dead. We were slaves to the world, to Satan, and to the passions of our own sinful nature. We were by nature objects of God's wrath. But God, in His great mercy and love, reached out to us and gave us spiritual life (see Ephesians 2:1-5). He forgave us our sins through the death of His Son and covered us with the spotless righteousness of Jesus Himself.

Christ's giving us spiritual life is a far greater miracle, and its benefits are infinitely greater than healing from leprosy. Yet how often do we give thanks for our salvation? Have you stopped today to give thanks to God for delivering you from the domain of darkness and transferring you to the kingdom of His Son? And if you have given thanks, was it in a mere nominal way, much like some people give thanks at a meal, or was it an expression of heartfelt gratitude for what God has done for you in Christ?

The truth is, our whole lives should be lives of continual thanksgiving. Paul told his audience at Athens that "[God] himself gives to all mankind life and breath and everything" (Acts 17:25). That means that every breath we draw is a gift from God. Everything we are and everything we have is a gift from Him. If you have intellectual or professional or technical skills, those skills are a gift from God. It's true you probably studied diligently in college and perhaps endured long hours of professional training, but where did the intellectual ability and innate talent that you have come from? They came from God, who created you with a built-in aptitude and then in His gracious providence directed you in the path of developing those skills.

We need to heed God's warning to the Israelites in Deuteronomy:

"Take care lest you forget the LORD your God by not keeping his commandments and his rules and his statutes, which I command you today, lest, when you have eaten and are full and have built good houses and live in them, and when your herds and flocks multiply and your silver and gold is multiplied and all that you have is multiplied, then your heart be lifted up, and you forget the LORD your God. . . . Beware lest you say in your heart, 'My power and the might of my hand have gotten me this wealth.' You shall remember the LORD your God, for it is he who gives you power to get wealth, that he may confirm his covenant that he swore to your fathers, as it is this day." (8:11-14,17-18)

Most people who read this book acknowledge that everything we have comes from God, but how often do we stop to give thanks to Him? At the end of a workday in your profession or job, do you ever take time to say, "Thank You, heavenly Father, for giving me the skill, ability, and health to do my work today"? Do you ever physically or mentally go through your house, look at your furnishings and various items of home decoration, and say to God, "Everything in the house and the food in the cupboard and the car (or cars) in the driveway are gifts from You. Thank You for Your gracious and generous provision"? And if you are still a student, do you ever give thanks to God for the intellectual ability and financial provision that enables you to prepare yourself for your future vocation? When you give thanks at mealtime, is it routine and perfunctory, or is it a heartfelt expression of your gratitude to God for His continual provision of all your physical needs?

Taking for granted all the temporal provisions and spiritual blessings that God has so richly bestowed on us, and so failing to continually give Him thanks, is one of our "acceptable" sins. In fact, far too many Christians wouldn't think of it as sin. Yet Paul, in his description of a Spirit-filled person, said we are to "[give] thanks always and for everything to God the Father in the name of our Lord Jesus Christ" (Ephesians 5:20). Note the words *always* and *everything*. That means our whole lives should be ones of continually giving thanks.

Giving thanks to God for both His temporal and spiritual blessings in our lives is not just a nice thing to do — it is the moral will of God. Failure to give Him the thanks due Him is sin. It may seem like a benign sin to us because it doesn't harm anyone else. But it is an affront and insult to the One who created us and sustains us every second of our lives. And if, as Jesus so clearly stated, loving God with all our heart, soul, and mind is the great and first commandment, then failure to give thanks to God as a habit of life is a violation of the greatest commandment.

In Romans 1:18-32, Paul gives a vivid description of the downward moral spiral of pagan humanity of that day, as God gave them up more and more to the wicked inclinations of their evil hearts. Near the beginning of that description, Paul writes, "Although they knew God, they did not honor him as God *or give thanks to him*, but they became futile in their thinking, and their foolish hearts were darkened" (verse 21, emphasis added).

So their ever-increasing wickedness actually began with their ungodliness (failure to honor God as God) and their unthankfulness to Him. Their actual moral degradation was a result of God's judgment on them as He progressively gave them up to greater and greater perverse forms of immorality and other evil expressions. We can easily discern from this section of Scripture that unthankfulness is a serious matter. It may seem like a small sin to us, but God takes it seriously.

Failure to honor God or give thanks to Him is obviously characteristic of present-day culture. And so is the increasing decadence of our age. In fact, the description of moral depravity (see Romans 1:24-32) could be applied to our age with hardly a change of words. One wonders if again it is God's judgment for failure to honor Him and give Him thanks. Surely, as believers we do not want to contribute to the occasion of God's judgment. But we do contribute if, along with society at large, we fail to give Him the thanks due Him. In fact, we may be more guilty because as believers we should know better. Jesus said, "Everyone to whom much was given, of him much will be required" (Luke 12:48). Because we believe that the Bible is the Word of God, we are more responsible to obey it. And part of our obedience is giving thanks to God always and for everything.

There is no question that the increasing moral decadence around us is appalling and scary. We often wonder how bad it will get. But the next time we judge these people we need to ask ourselves if we have in some way contributed to their downward spiral into moral corruption through our own failure, along with theirs, to honor God and give Him thanks.

So we should give thanks always and for everything. We should especially give thanks when we have experienced an unusual provision from God or deliverance from some difficult circumstance. In session 4 I confess my temptation to anxiety when I face the possibility of missing a flight connection. A related air travel temptation to anxiety occurs at the baggage claim area when I wonder if my checked luggage arrived with me on my flight. I have had so many delayed-bag incidents that I never assume anymore that my bag has arrived with me. That's why the temptation to anxiety occurs. So I have to review the truths about anxiety in chapter 9 every time I go to baggage claim.

While working on this chapter, I flew to São Paulo, Brazil, for some ministry opportunities. Upon arrival, and after clearing immigration control, I went to the baggage claim area along with more than 150 other passengers from my flight, where once again I had to deal with my anxiety temptation. The pressure began to build as more and more bags came along the conveyor belt, and mine was not among them. (A delayed bag can especially become a problem in a foreign country.) After about two-thirds of the passengers had retrieved their luggage, mine finally appeared. As I pulled it off the conveyor belt, I lifted a heartfelt prayer of thanksgiving to God. And then as I unpacked in my hotel room, I again thanked God that I had the bag there to unpack.

A delayed-bag incident may seem trivial to you, and, in the course of a lifetime, it is. But when you have to wear the same clothes for two or three days and have to buy replacement toilet articles, it doesn't seem so trivial at the time. But the truth is that life is full of events that delay us, inconvenience us, or obstruct or block some plan of ours. In the midst of these events, we should fight against anxiety and frustration. But when God does bring relief, or when we see Him deliver us from the possibility of such an event, we should make it a special point to give Him thanks.

## IN ALL CIRCUMSTANCES?

Let's pursue the baggage claim scenario a bit further. Suppose my bag had not arrived with me on the flight, or even suppose it never arrived. Am I to still give God thanks? Before we look at the answer to that question, mentally insert into this story some predicament of your own, either an actual event or some imaginary one you hope never happens. This will help keep the following answer to the question from being theoretical; that is, in your own situation, whether real or theoretical, should you give God thanks?

So the question is, *Are we to give God thanks when the circumstances do not turn out as we had hoped?* The answer is yes, but for a different reason. In 1 Thessalonians 5:18, Paul writes, "Give thanks in all circumstances; for this is the will of God in Christ Jesus for you."

This command is different from the command in Ephesians 5:20, where we are to give thanks to God for everything. I believe, considering the context, that in Ephesians, Paul is exhorting us to develop a habit of continual thanksgiving for all the blessings God so graciously pours out on us; that is, one characteristic of a Spirit-filled life is a thankful heart.

In the Thessalonians passage, however, Paul is instructing us to give thanks *in* all circumstances, even those we would not *feel* thankful about. Is Paul asking us to give thanks through gritted teeth by sheer willpower when in our heart of hearts we are truly disappointed? The answer to the question lies in the promises of God found in Romans 8:28-29 and 38-39:

> We know that for those who love God all things work together for good, for those who are called according to his purpose. For those whom he foreknew he also predestined to be conformed to the image of his Son, in order that he might be the firstborn among many brothers. . . . For I am sure that neither death nor life, nor angels nor rulers, nor things present nor things to come, nor powers, nor height nor depth, nor anything else in all creation, will be able to separate us from the love of God in Christ Jesus our Lord.

Verse 28 tells us that for those who love God, all things work together for good. The meaning is that *God causes* all things to work together for good; for "things" — that is, circumstances — do not work together for good themselves. Rather, God directs the outcome of those circumstances for our good. The "good," however, is defined in verse 29 as our being conformed to the image of God's Son. In other words, Paul is telling us that God intends all our circumstances, both good and bad (but in the context Paul has in mind, especially the bad ones), to be instruments of sanctification, of growing us more and more into the likeness of Jesus.

So in situations that do not turn out the way we hoped, we are to give God thanks that He will use the situation in some way to develop our Christian character. We don't need to speculate as to *how* He might use it, for His ways are often mysterious and beyond our understanding. So *by faith* in the promise of God in Romans 8:28-29, we obey the command of 1 Thessalonians 5:18 to give thanks in the circumstances.

Further, as we are in the midst of the difficult circumstance, we have the promise of verses 38-39 that nothing, including the situation we are in, can separate us from the love of God. Again we must cling to this promise by faith. So we have a dual assurance to enable us to give thanks in the circumstance. First, by faith we believe God is using or will use the particular difficulty to conform us more to Jesus. Second, we have the assurance that even in the midst of the difficulty we are enveloped in God's love.

So the giving of thanks in a disappointing or difficult situation is always to be done by faith in the promises of God. It is not a matter of doing it by sheer willpower. If we do that, we are giving thanks with our lips but not with our hearts. But as we cling to the promises of God, we can say, "Father, the circumstance I am in now is difficult and painful. I would not have chosen it, but You in Your love and wisdom chose it for me. You intend it for my good, and so by faith I thank You for the good You are going to do in my life through it. Help me to genuinely believe this and be able to thank You from my heart."

So in summary, we should seek to develop the habit of continually giving thanks to God. We should above all thank Him for our salvation and for the opportunities we have for spiritual growth and ministry. We should thank Him frequently for the abundance of material blessings He has provided. And then, when circumstances go awry and do not turn out the way we had hoped, we should, by faith, thank Him for what He is doing in the circumstances to transform us more and more into the likeness of His Son.

As an application of this chapter — to develop the habit of giving thanks — I suggest memorizing Ephesians 5:20 and 1 Thessalonians 5:18 and regularly praying over them, asking God to work them out in your life. This way you will grow more and more in the habit of giving thanks always and for everything. Then in your time with God each day, spend part of the time giving thanks for specific temporal and spiritual blessings.

Now let's return again to the primary purpose of this book. As the subtitle suggests, it's to help us honestly confront the subtle sins we tolerate in our own lives so that we will tend to walk more humbly before God and with respect to the unbelievers toward whom we may be so judgmental. This purpose will be met only to the extent that we all, including myself, prayerfully examine our hearts and lives before God, asking Him to show us our own subtle sins. In fact, I hope you did that earlier in this session at the end of chapter 7, and will continue to do so in the following sessions.

If by now you are already discouraged about your sins, remember the gospel. Though your obedience to God's law is defiled and imperfect, Christ's obedience is perfect and complete. And God has not only forgiven you your sins (both the subtle and the not-so-subtle) but has also credited to you that spotless obedience of Christ. God does want to work in you and with you to deal with your sins, but He does so as your Father, not your Judge.

If you've not been fazed by anything in this session, then you need to look back through it again. Are you sure you are not to some degree ungodly? Is your life entirely focused on God, so that you see all of life from that perspective? What about unthankfulness? Do you thank God always and for everything, and do you thank Him *in* the difficult circumstances you experience?

77

Notes and Observations

Hopefully by now all of us have realized we do have some "respectable" sins, perhaps attitudes and actions we've never regarded as sin or realized their seriousness. If you have been humbled to some degree and your heart made more tender, then you are in a good position to continue on, because the sins we look at from here on will probably be more "ugly" than the ones we've examined so far.

# Ungodliness and Unthankfulness

## (Chapters 7 and 8)

## STUDY QUESTIONS

KEY VERSES: "The grace of God has appeared, bringing salvation for all people, training us to renounce ungodliness.... Be filled with the Spirit, ... giving thanks always and for everything to God the Father in the name of our Lord Jesus Christ." (Titus 2:11-12; Ephesians 5:18,20)

## GET FOCUSED

*Ungodliness* is at the root of other "respectable" sins. All of us, to some degree, are ungodly. We live, at least occasionally, with little or no conscious thought of God — of God's will, God's glory, our dependence on God, or our responsibility to God. We forget that we live in the presence of the all-seeing, all-hearing God, who longs to be in intimate relationship with us.

Fortunately, God shows us how to deal with ungodliness. He wants us to glorify Him, to live lives worthy of Him and pleasing to Him — to let our light shine before others so they, too, may give glory to Him (see Matthew 5:16). He wants us to prayerfully desire an intimate relationship with Him that will permeate everything we think, say, and do. In this session, you'll learn about living in the awareness that all you are, have, and accomplish is by God's grace.

The other sin we'll examine today is *unthankfulness* toward God — not thanking Him for the many blessings He bestows on us, such as salvation, deliverance from spiritual darkness, and the gift of life. Everything we are and have is a gift from Him.

Even the ancient Israelites forgot to thank God for His spiritual and provisional blessings ... with dire results. No wonder the apostle Paul wrote that we are to "[give] thanks always and for everything to God the Father in the name of our Lord Jesus Christ" (Ephesians 5:20). A spirit of thankfulness can transform your life!

## THINK IT THROUGH
## FOR PERSONAL STUDY

### I. Dealing with the Sin of Ungodliness

1. How is the definition of *ungodliness* on pages 61–62 different from what you thought *ungodliness* meant? What does Romans 1:18 reveal about this sin?

2. Do you agree or disagree that ungodliness is "apt to be the root cause of our other sins" and that each of us is guilty of this sin? Explain your answer.

3. Read James 4:13-15. For what expression of ungodliness did James, through the Holy Spirit, condemn those people?

4. What does Paul's summary prayer (Colossians 1:9-10) reveal about our responsibility to God? About our "typical," human-centered prayers for ourselves, friends, and family members?

## II. *Dealing with the Sin of Unthankfulness*

1. During biblical times, leprosy devastated many lives. The Mosaic Law required that a leper continually cry out, "unclean, unclean" while walking along the road (Leviticus 13:45). In light of this, what is poignant about Jesus' experience between Samaria and Galilee? (See Luke 17:11-19.)

2. Read Romans 6:6,17 and Ephesians 2:1-5.

   a. What is a person's spiritual condition without God?

   b. What has God done for every believer?

3. According to Acts 17:24-25, why should we express heartfelt gratitude to God?

4. According to the promises of Romans 8:28-29,38-39, why should we give thanks by faith even when a situation is disappointing or difficult?

## TALK IT OVER
## FOR GROUP DISCUSSION

1. Why do you think it's so easy for good people to be ungodly — to live most of the week as if God doesn't exist, as if they are not responsible to Him and dependent on Him?

2. If you feel comfortable doing so, share a time when you went through daily activities without even thinking of God. What impact did it have on your life or on those around you?

3. What practical things can we do each day to "train" ourselves "for godliness" (1 Timothy 4:7) so we please and glorify God during even ordinary activities?

4. What are some blessings God has given you? Why is it important for us to thank Him for these blessings and make such thankfulness a natural part of our lives?

5. Review Romans 1:18-32, in which Paul vividly describes the downward moral spiral of pagan humanity. In verse 21, what does he emphasize regarding thankfulness, and what conclusions might we draw from this regarding our lives? Our culture?

6. Where does the faith come from to believe and thank God even in the midst of difficult circumstances? Describe a challenging time when you were — or were not — able to give thanks. What did God teach you through that experience?

## GROUP PRAYER

As a group, ask God to kindle within each of you an even stronger desire to live a lifestyle of godliness and thankfulness.

❧ ❧

FOR NEXT TIME: Read *Respectable Sins* chapters 9 and 10, and then answer the questions in the "Think It Through" personal-study section for session 4.

# TAKE IT TO HEART
*A Personal-Growth Journal*

### *Personal Reflection*

Reread 1 Corinthians 10:31 and Matthew 5:16. To what extent are you mindful of doing "all" to the glory of God? How has ungodliness crept (or marched) into your social relationships . . . ordinary activities . . . your prayers . . . daily planning?

Do your words and actions demonstrate that you consciously and prayerfully seek to glorify God — or tend to forget about Him? What are your attitudes and actions communicating?

How much has God done for you in Christ? In what ways can you be sure to take time each day to thank God for His temporal provisions and spiritual blessings?

### *Personal Action Point*

If God stood in front of you right now and told you to do *everything* to His glory, what changes would you immediately make in order to make Him the center focal point of your life?

### *Personal Prayer*

Write out a brief prayer of commitment to the personal action points you listed above.

---

## PROGRESS REPORT

How well did you do at consciously thinking about God? What helped you be more mindful of Him — His blessings, His will, His glory, your dependence on Him?

To what extent were you thankful to God — for unpleasant as well as great circumstances?

What challenges did you face in cultivating an attitude of thankfulness?

# Anxiety, Frustration, and Discontentment

BEFORE GATHERING: Read the following portion of *Respectable Sins*. In the margins, record observations, illustrations, or questions that come to mind as you read. Then answer the "Think It Through" study questions that follow the reading.

---

## Chapter Nine: Anxiety and Frustration

Notes and Observations

Life is often difficult, and sometimes painful. If my car breaks down on a vacation trip, that is difficult. If I have an accident and am permanently disabled, that is painful. And of course there are varying degrees of difficulty and, to some extent, of pain. Difficulties usually occur in the ordinary activities and responsibilities of life, whereas pain is likely generated by extraordinary events. So in this chapter we're going to focus on the difficulties of ordinary life and our too-frequent responses to those difficulties in the forms of anxiety and frustration.

## ANXIETY

Some years ago, I surveyed the entire New Testament looking for instances where various Christian character traits were taught by precept or by example. I found twenty-seven. It may not surprise you that *love* was taught most often, some fifty times. It may surprise you that *humility* was a close second with forty instances. But what really surprised me is that *trust in God* in all our circumstances was third, being taught thirteen or more times.

The opposite of trust in God is either anxiety or frustration, and Jesus had a lot to say about anxiety. The most prominent passage in which Jesus speaks about it is Matthew 6:25-34, in which He uses the word *anxious* six times. We are not to be anxious about what we are to eat, drink, or wear, or even about the unknown circumstances of tomorrow. Another expression Jesus uses regarding anxiety is "Fear not" or, as some translations render it, "Do not be afraid" (see, for example, Matthew 10:31; Luke 12:7). Paul picks up this admonition about anxiety with his words in Philippians 4:6, "Do not be anxious about anything." And Peter adds his exhortation, "[Cast] all your anxieties on him, because he cares for you" (1 Peter 5:7).

When you or I say to someone, "Don't be anxious" or "Don't be afraid," we are simply trying to encourage the person, or admonish in a helpful way. But when Jesus (or Paul or Peter, who were writing under divine inspiration) says to us, "Don't be anxious," it has the force of a moral command. In other words, it is the moral will of God that we not be anxious. Or to say it more explicitly, *anxiety is sin.*

Anxiety is sin for two reasons. First, as I've already mentioned, anxiety is a distrust of God. In the Matthew 6:25-34 passage, Jesus said that if our heavenly Father takes care of the birds of the air and the lilies of the field, will He not much more take care of our temporal needs? And Peter told us that the basis of our casting our anxieties on God is that He cares for us. So when I give way to anxiety, I am, in effect, believing that God does not care for me and that He will not take care of me in the particular circumstance that triggers my anxiety of the moment.

Suppose someone you love were to say to you, "I don't trust you. I don't believe you love me and will care for me." What an affront that would be to you! Yet that is what we are saying to God by our anxiety.

Anxiety is a sin also because it is a lack of acceptance of God's providence in our lives. God's providence may be simply defined as God's orchestrating all circumstances and events in His universe for His glory and the good of His people. Some believers have difficulty accepting the fact that God does in fact orchestrate all events and circumstances, and even those of us who do believe it often lose sight of this glorious truth. Instead we tend to focus on the immediate causes of our anxiety rather than remembering that those immediate causes are under the sovereign control of God.

I have to confess that anxiety is one of my most persistent temptations. It's not that I'm a Chicken Little who is always afraid the sky is falling. Rather, my most common temptation to anxiety occurs in connection with air travel, which I do frequently. Almost always, my travel to another city involves connecting flights at one of the airline's hub cities. Often my first flight from the city where I live to the hub is late, resulting in a tight connection to the second flight. So I am tempted to become anxious. Will I make my connection to my destination city? And usually I am scheduled to speak within a few hours after my scheduled arrival, so it's important to me that I make that flight. (Obviously, in the course of a lifetime, or compared to other people's problems, this is a minor issue, but for me at the time, it is a major one.)

So my agenda is to arrive at my destination city on time and get comfortably settled before I am to speak. But what if God's agenda is different? What if God's agenda is for me to be late for that meeting, or miss it altogether? (I have had both experiences.) Will I succumb to the temptation to anxiety and fret and fume, or will I believe that God is in sovereign control of my travel and accept *His* agenda, whatever that may be? As I have struggled with anxiety in this area of life, I have come to the conclusion that my anxiety is triggered not so much by a distrust in God as by an unwillingness to submit to and cheerfully accept His agenda for me.

I tend to think, *Lord, it's important that I arrive in time to speak at that meeting. The people in charge are counting on me. What will they do if I don't arrive in time?* But I have learned to say to myself, *But God, it's Your meeting. If You don't want me there, that's Your business. And what the people who are counting on me to be there will do is also Your business. God, I*

Notes and Observations

*accept Your agenda for this situation, whatever that may be.*

I have been greatly helped in this issue of accepting God's providential will, or God's agenda, as I often call it, by the writings of John Newton, whom we've already encountered in session 2 (chapter 4). In one of his letters to a friend, Newton wrote:

> [One of the marks of Christian maturity which a believer should seek is] an acquiescence in the Lord's will founded in a persuasion of his wisdom, holiness, sovereignty, and goodness. . . . So far as we attain to this, we are secure from disappointment. Our own limited views, and short-sighted purposes and desires, may be, and will be, often over-ruled; but then our main and leading desire, that the will of the Lord may be done, must be accomplished. How highly does it become us, both as creatures and as sinners, to submit to the appointments of our Maker! and how necessary is it to our peace! This great attainment is too often unthought of, and over-looked; we are prone to fix our attention upon the second causes and immediate instruments of events; forgetting that whatever befalls us is according to his purpose, and therefore must be right and seasonable in itself, and shall in the issue be productive of good. From hence arise impatience, resentment, and secret repinings [i.e., complainings], which are not only sinful, but tormenting; whereas, if all things are in his hand, if the very hairs of our head are numbered; if every event, great and small, is under the direction of his providence and purpose; and if he has a wise, holy, and gracious end in view, to which everything that happens is subordinate and subservient; — then we have nothing to do, but with patience and humility to follow as he leads, and cheerfully to expect a happy issue. . . . How happy are they who can resign all to him, see his hand in every dispensation,

and believe that he chooses better for them than they possibly could for themselves![1]

An acceptance of God's providential will does not mean we are not to pray about the eventual outcome. Paul's command to not be anxious is accompanied by the instruction to pray about whatever situation is tempting us to be anxious (see Philippians 4:6). And Jesus, in dread of His impending suffering on the cross, which far exceeded any anxiety we will ever experience, prayed, "If it be possible, let this cup pass from me; nevertheless, not as I will, but as you will" (Matthew 26:39). So it is appropriate to pray for relief and for deliverance from whatever circumstance is triggering our anxiety, but we should always do so with an attitude of acceptance of whatever God's providential will may be and a confidence that, whatever the outcome, God's will is better than our plans or desires.[2]

You may or may not be frequently tempted to anxiety as I am. But if you are, can you recognize the types of circumstances that tend to make you anxious? Do you identify with me in chafing under God's providential will for you when it is different from your own agenda? If so, I encourage you to memorize and pray over some of the texts I have mentioned in this chapter, especially in connection with any recurring circumstances you identify that tend to trigger your anxiety. Above all, ask God to give you faith to believe that His providential will for you in these circumstances comes to you from His infinite wisdom and goodness and is ultimately intended for your good. And then ask God to give you a heart that is submissive to His providential will when it is contrary to your own plans.

## WORRY

Worry is a synonym for anxiety. While some translations of Matthew 6:25-34 speak of *anxiety*, the New International Version uses the word *worry*. In popular usage, however, we tend to associate worry with more long-term difficult or painful circumstances for which there appears to be no resolution. These are the kinds of circumstances that tend to keep a person awake at night "worrying" about what to do while realizing there is nothing one can do.

For example, I have several friends who have mentally or physically dependent adult children. These friends can easily lie awake at night worrying about the future for their child after both husband and wife die. Even if finances were not a factor, which it is for all of my friends, the question remains, *Who will care for my child?*

These are indeed difficult circumstances, and I have to be careful here because I have not experienced any such seemingly intractable situation. So I do not mean to dismiss lightly these circumstances, but if we want to stick closely to Scripture, we have no choice but to seek to do what it says. And in the New International Version, Jesus says, "Therefore do not worry about tomorrow" (Matthew 6:34).

We do have the promises of God and the ministry of the Holy Spirit to help us in these difficult times. Recently, a friend, who is actually experiencing one of these long-term situations, called my attention to the Phillips Modern English rendering of 1 Peter 5:7, "You can throw the whole weight of your anxieties upon him, for you are his personal concern." Though the Phillips version is usually regarded as a paraphrase, I believe its rendering of 1 Peter 5:7 accurately captures the meaning of the text. Jesus said that God does not forget a single sparrow (see Luke 12:6). How much more, then, is it true that you, His child, are indeed His personal concern?

It's true, however, that oftentimes the situation at hand looms larger in our minds than the promises of God. We then find it difficult to believe the promises. In those times, I find the words of the father of a demon-possessed son encouraging: "I believe; help my unbelief!" (Mark 9:24). There is a vast difference between stubborn unbelief such as was demonstrated by

SESSION FOUR: Anxiety, Frustration, and Discontentment

the people of Jesus' hometown, Nazareth (see Mark 6:5-6), and the struggling faith of the son's father. God honors our struggles, and the Holy Spirit will help us. The important issue is that we seek to honor God through our faith, even though weak and faltering, rather than dishonoring Him through rank unbelief.

## FRUSTRATION

Closely akin to anxiety or worry is the sin of frustration. Whereas anxiety involves fear, frustration usually involves being upset or even angry at whatever or whoever is blocking our plans. I might have an important document to print from my computer, but the printer will only produce gobbledygook. Instead of believing that God is sovereignly in control over the actions of my computer and that He has a good reason for allowing it to act up, I get frustrated. Actually, this type of reaction has its roots in my ungodliness at the moment, for at that time I am living as though God is not involved in my life or my circumstances. I fail to recognize the invisible hand of God behind whatever is triggering my frustration. In the heat of the moment, I tend not to think about God at all. Instead, I focus entirely on the immediate cause of my frustration.

The passage of Scripture that has greatly helped me deal with frustration is Psalm 139:16, which says, "All the days ordained for me were written in your book before one of them came to be" (NIV). "Days ordained for me" refers not only to the length of my life but to all the events and circumstances of each day of my life. This is a tremendously encouraging and comforting thought. So when something happens that tends to frustrate me, I actually quote Psalm 139:16 to myself and then say to God, "This circumstance is part of Your plan for my life today. Help me to respond in faith and in a God-honoring way to Your providential will. And then please give me wisdom to know how to address the situation that tends to cause the frustration."

91

Note what resources I have brought to bear on the circumstance that tends to frustrate me: specific applicable Scripture and dependence on the Holy Spirit expressed through prayer to enable me to respond in a godly manner. And then I pray for practical wisdom to know how to deal with the situation. After all, in my illustration about the computer printer, the important document does eventually need to be printed.

It is also beneficial to ask God if there is something I need to learn, or if there is something I need to be attentive to. Sometimes God uses events that tempt us toward frustration to get our attention, or even to push us further in an area we need to grow in. In any case, there are no events in our lives that do not ultimately come to us from the invisible hand of God, even though they come through some visible cause.

Let me repeat, however, what I have said or implied throughout this chapter. Both anxiety and frustration are sins. They are not to be taken lightly or brushed off as common reactions we have to difficult events in a fallen world. Can you picture Jesus ever being anxious or frustrated? And whatever in our lives is not like Jesus is sin. Granted, we will never achieve complete freedom from anxiety or frustration in this life (at least I don't expect to). But we should never accept them as just part of our temperament any more than we would accept adultery as part of our temperament. Keep in mind that even though anxiety and frustration may not be as serious as adultery, they are still sins. And all sin is serious in the eyes of a Holy God.

## Chapter Ten: Discontentment

Anxiety is a fearful uncertainty over the future, whether short-term (as in my plane trips) or long-term, such as might result from a job loss. Frustration is usually the result of some immediate event that has blocked my plans or desires. Discontentment, the subject of this chapter, most often arises from ongoing and unchanging circumstances that we can do nothing about.

Before we get into the subject, however, I want to acknowledge that there is a place for legitimate discontentment. All of us should, to some degree, be discontent with our spiritual growth. If we are not, we will stop growing. There is also what we might call a prophetic discontentment with injustice and other evils in society that is coupled with a desire to see positive change. The subject of this chapter is a sinful discontentment that negatively affects our relationship with God.

Actually, the most frequent warnings in Scripture against discontentment concern money and possessions, but in this chapter, I want to address what is perhaps a more common form of discontentment among committed Christians, an attitude that may be triggered by unchanging circumstances that are trials to our faith.

Here are some examples of such unchanging circumstances:

- An unfulfilling or low-paying job
- Singleness well into midlife or beyond
- Inability to bear children
- An unhappy marriage
- Physical disabilities
- Continual poor health

I'm sure there are other painful circumstances I haven't included in this list. But whatever they are, the truths of this chapter will apply to them all.

In addition to the really painful circumstances of life, the cause of our discontentment may even be trivial at times. I am not good at administrative details, so having to constantly deal with them can become an emotional leak for me and thus a temptation to be discontent. Obviously, the necessity of having to handle administrative details is trivial compared to any of the areas I've listed above. But I mention it to point out that however good our overall circumstances may be, there is often some small thing over which we can become discontent.

It's not that I am unacquainted with some of those more difficult areas. I was almost thirty-four when I got married, so I know something of the loneliness of single adult life. And even after marriage I struggled with discontentment at our son's soccer or basketball games because I was at least ten years older than the other parents around me. And then there are the physical disabilities. All my life I have had both a visual and a hearing disability, neither of which is treatable. I can remember the feeling of rejection as I was growing up when, because of my visual disability, I could not play baseball like the other boys. Still today, even as an older adult, those lifetime disabilities often make life inconvenient, if not difficult.

I don't intend that last paragraph to sound like a pity party. And I readily recognize that the circumstances I deal with are minor indeed compared to what many believers experience. But I do want you to know that if you struggle with discontentment, I'm right there with you. Your circumstances may be much more difficult than any I've ever experienced, but the truth is, it is our response to our circumstances rather than the degree of difficulty that determines whether or not we are discontent.

Whatever situation tempts us to be discontent, and however severe it may be, we need to recognize that discontentment is sin. That statement may surprise many readers. We are so used to responding to difficult circumstances with anxiety, frustration, or discontentment that we consider them normal reactions to the varying vicissitudes of life. But if we tend to think this way, that just points out to us the subtleness and acceptability of these sins. When we fail to recognize these responses to our circumstances as sin, we are responding no differently from unbelievers who never factor God into their situations. We are back to our ungodliness as the root cause of our sins.

Notes and Observations

The primary purpose of this book is to help us face the presence of many of these subtle sins in our lives and to recognize the fact that, to a large degree, they have become acceptable to us. We tolerate them in our lives with hardly a second thought. That makes them more dangerous because, in addition to the basic sin itself, they can open the door of our hearts to greater sin. Discontentment, for example, can easily lead to resentment or bitterness toward God or other people.

The second purpose of the book is to suggest means of dealing with these sins, even though these sections are admittedly brief. And you will find as we go through these sessions that, for me, appropriate passages of Scripture are my first line of attack. After all, in His High Priestly prayer, Jesus prayed, "Sanctify them in the truth; your word is truth" (John 17:17). While the "word of truth" probably refers primarily to the gospel, it certainly includes the truth of God's moral will throughout Scripture as well as the words of instruction and encouragement that help us obey that moral will.

I have already mentioned Psalm 139:16 as a passage of Scripture that helps me with frustration. But the same truth that God has ordained all our days, with all their ups and downs, their blessings and disappointments, can help us (and does help me) deal with the circumstances that tempt us to be discontent. Whatever your circumstances, and however difficult they may be, the truth is that they are ordained by God for you as part of His overall plan for your life. God does nothing, or allows nothing, without a purpose. And His purposes, however mysterious and inscrutable they may be to us, are always for His glory and our ultimate good.

And for those of us who face physical disabilities or even physical appearance issues, Psalm 139:13 can help us. "You formed my inward parts; you knitted me together in my mother's womb." God so directed the DNA and other biological factors that determine our physical makeup that the psalmist can say, "God formed me in my mother's womb." That is an incredible thought! You and I are who we are physically because that is the way God made us. And He made us the way we are because that is how we can best fulfill His plan for our lives. For some with severe disabilities, that plan may at times seem meaningless. But if we believe that we are who we are and what we are because that is the way God made us, then we can learn to accept our disabilities and believe that He can even use them to glorify Himself.

Psalm 139:13 can be helpful to those of us who experience some degree of physical limitation. Obviously, there are many other areas of life that would not be addressed by this text. But you can be sure that you will be able to find in the Bible specific texts or principles that will address your particular circumstances.

Years ago a friend gave me a poem by Amy Carmichael titled "In Acceptance Lieth Peace." In the first four verses Amy Carmichael portrays the suffering speaker in the poem as seeking peace in forgetting, in restless endeavor, in aloofness, and even in submission to the inevitable. Finally in the fifth verse the sufferer finds relief in these words:

> He said, "I will accept the breaking sorrow
> Which God to-morrow
> Will to His son explain."
> Then did the turmoil deep within him cease,
> *Not vain the word; not vain:*
> *For in Acceptance lieth peace.*[3]

One avenue of dealing with disappointing circumstances that Amy Carmichael did not cover is that of resignation, which can often be done grudgingly because we have no choice. We can resign ourselves to circumstances we know will never change but still harbor in our hearts a smoldering discontentment. But as Amy Carmichael so helpfully brought out, it is neither in resignation nor submission but only in acceptance that we find peace.

Acceptance means that you accept your circumstances from God, trusting that He unerringly knows what is best for you and that in His love, He purposes only that which is best. Having then reached a state of acceptance, you can ask God to let you use your difficult circumstances to glorify Him. In this way you have moved from the attitude of a victim to an attitude of stewardship. You begin to ask, "God, how can I use my disability (or whatever the difficult circumstance may be) to serve You and glorify You?"

You may ask, "But shouldn't I pray for physical healing or for relief from any other painful circumstance?" Yes, we are invited to pray about these circumstances, but we should always pray in confidence that our infinitely wise and loving heavenly Father knows what is best for us, and we should be willing to accept His answer to us.

After the death of my first wife, a friend sent me a card with the following anonymous quote:

Lord, I am willing to —
Receive what you give,
Lack what you withhold,
Relinquish what you take.

Obviously, at the time, the thought of being willing to relinquish my wife was the message appropriate for me. But if through an accident you become totally disabled, could you say, "Lord, I am willing to receive this crippling disability You have given me"? If you are single with no prospects of marriage, can you say, "Lord, I am willing to lack what You have withheld"?

Some years ago, I experienced a crushing and humiliating disappointment. At the time, I didn't know the little anonymous verse I've just quoted, but I did know Job 1:21: "[Job] said, 'Naked I came from my mother's womb, and naked shall I return. The Lord gave, and the Lord has taken away; blessed be the name of the Lord.'" The morning after the event, I knelt

97

before the Lord and said, "Lord, You gave and You have taken away; blessed be Your name." Through that Scripture and that prayer, God enabled me to relinquish what He had taken. I did not know at the time that that experience was a trial run for the far greater challenge of relinquishing my wife several years later.

You will recognize that there is a recurring theme running through this session. That theme is the importance of a firm belief in the sovereignty, wisdom, and goodness of God in all the circumstances of our lives.[4] Whether those circumstances are short-term or long-term, our ability to respond to them in a God-honoring and God-pleasing manner depends on our ability and willingness to bring these truths to bear on them. And we must do this by faith; that is, we must believe that the Bible's teaching about these attributes really is true and that God has brought or allowed these difficult circumstances in our lives for His glory and our ultimate good.

Finally, I realize that in dealing with discontentment, I probably have touched some raw nerves. And this may be especially aggravated when I label discontentment as sin. You may be thinking, *If he only knew my situation, he wouldn't be so glib and "preachy."* It's true, I don't know your situation, but I write as one who has struggled with discontentment and has sought to overcome it with the truths I have set forth in this chapter. They have helped me, and I pray they will help you. May all of us, with the help of the Holy Spirit, move from any negative attitudes of discontentment to a positive attitude of being stewards of the difficult and disappointing circumstances God has given us so that we may somehow glorify Him in all of life.

# Anxiety, Frustration, and Discontentment

## (Chapters 9 and 10)

## STUDY QUESTIONS

KEY VERSES: "[Cast] all your anxieties on him [God], because he cares for you. . . . All the days ordained for me were written in your book before one of them came to be." (1 Peter 5:7; Psalm 139:16, NIV)

## GET FOCUSED

Each of us experiences pain and difficulties. Cars break down. Accidents hurt us or those we love. Relationships sour. Certainly you could list many examples. During this session, we'll consider three common "respectable" sins that often surface during painful or difficult times — anxiety, frustration, discontentment — and their considerable impact.

*Anxiety* (sometimes translated *worry*) shows up frequently in the Bible. Jesus often spoke about anxiety — once using this word six times in ten verses (See Matthew 6:25-34). ("Sister" words also show up often: "fear" and "afraid.") Why is anxiety — a fearful uncertainty over the future — among the "respectable" sins we're examining? Because when we are anxious, we distrust God *and* we don't accept His sovereign orchestration of circumstances and events. We chafe under His providential will for our lives when it is different from our agendas.

*Frustration* usually involves becoming upset or even angry at whatever or whoever blocks our plans or desires. We forget that God's invisible hand is behind whatever triggers our frustration. As we'll see, whenever we face frustration we can rely on key resources and probably need to learn to pay attention to certain things.

### If, Then

If all things are in his [God's] hand, if the very hairs of our head are numbered; if every event, great and small, is under the direction of his providence and purpose; and if he has a wise, holy, and gracious end in view . . . then we have nothing to do but with patience and humility to follow as he leads, and cheerfully to expect a happy issue.

JOHN NEWTON,
*Letters of Newton*[5]

*Discontentment*, which often arises from ongoing and unchanging circumstances we can do nothing about, is sinful when it negatively affects our relationship with God. How do we respond to Him when a job or marriage doesn't work out, we remain childless, chronic pain continues, or we face burdensome administrative details?

With the Holy Spirit's help, not only can we deal effectively with these sins as they crop up, but we can also experience more of God — and learn to trust Him no matter what circumstances we face.

## THINK IT THROUGH
## FOR PERSONAL STUDY

### I. Anxiety and Frustration

1. What did Jesus teach, in Matthew 6:25-34, about how believers should respond to anxiety (worry)?

2. What do Matthew 26:39 and Philippians 4:6-7 reveal about our need to pray for relief and deliverance from whatever tempts us to be anxious?

3. When our faith falters and our situations loom larger in our minds than God's promises, how should we obey Jesus' command in Matthew 6:34 and find hope in Luke 12:6? What insight does Mark 9:23-24 offer?

4. Our frustration, which usually involves being upset at whatever or whoever blocks our plans or desires, has roots in ungodliness because we are living as if God is not involved in our circumstances. What comforting and encouraging insights can we gain from Psalm 139:16 (NIV): "All the days ordained for me were written in your [God's] book before one of them came to be"?

## II. Discontentment

1. What is discontentment? When does it spur us to positive action — and when is it sinful?

2. Jerry writes, "It is our response to our circumstances rather than the degree of difficulty [in them] that determines whether or not we are discontent." Do you agree or disagree? Why?

3. One of the key verses for this session is Psalm 139:16. How might this verse help us in dealing with circumstances that tempt us to be discontented?

4. Write out what this statement from the author means to you: "We must believe that the Bible's teaching about these attributes [God's sovereignty, wisdom, goodness] really is true and that God has brought or allowed these difficult circumstances in our lives for His glory and our ultimate good."

## TALK IT OVER
### FOR GROUP DISCUSSION

1. Why is anxiety so common in our culture — in our daily activities, in advertising, in news reports? How does the Bible's teaching about anxiety contradict what modern culture teaches about it?

2. Which other sins often crop up if we tolerate anxiety, frustration, and/or discontentment in our lives?

3. Do you think God sometimes allows us to face difficult, unchanging circumstances for reasons we may never know? Feel free to share a situation in which you learned a key lesson because you accepted that situation as part of God's plan for your life.

4. Discuss this quote from the author: "Suppose someone you love were to say to you, 'I don't trust you. I don't believe you love me and will care for me.' What an affront that would be to you! Yet that is what we are saying to God by our anxiety."

5. Throughout *Respectable Sins*, Jerry encourages us to remember God's attributes. If we believe and remember that God is infinitely wise, loving, and knows what is best for us, then how will we respond to circumstances that tempt us to be anxious, frustrated, and discontented? On the other hand, if we think God is simply toying with us and wanting us to suffer, how will we respond to trials?

## GROUP PRAYER

In group prayer, thank God for making each of you more aware of "respectable" sins and their impact on your lives and relationships. Ask God for faith to believe that His providential will for you in all circumstances comes from His infinite wisdom and goodness — and is ultimately intended for your good.

❧ ❧

FOR NEXT TIME: Read *Respectable Sins* chapters 11 and 12, and then respond to the questions in the "Think It Through" personal-study section for session 5.

## TAKE IT TO HEART
### *A PERSONAL-GROWTH JOURNAL*

### *Personal Reflection*

What types of circumstances tempt you to become anxious, frustrated, and/or discontented?

When has God used your anxiety, frustration, and/or discontentment to teach you something, help you grow in a particular area, or get your attention and make you more attentive?

Which particular insights, quotations, or verses in session 4 especially connected with you? Why?

### *Personal Action Point*

This next week, carefully note which circumstances tempt you to be anxious, frustrated, or discontented, and when temptation occurs, immediately ask God to help you trust and obey Him.

### *Personal Prayer*

Write a prayer thanking God for being in control of your circumstances (even when you don't *feel* that certainty). Invite Him to help you respond in ways that serve and glorify Him.

---

## PROGRESS REPORT

Since the last session, how did you do at trusting God with your anxieties and accepting His sovereign will?

If you became frustrated or discontented, what steps did you take? Or, what steps *should* you have taken?

In which specific area(s) have you noted progress?

# Pride and Selfishness

BEFORE GATHERING: Read the following portion of *Respectable Sins*. In the margins, record observations, illustrations, or questions that come to mind as you read. Then answer the "Think It Through" study questions that follow the reading.

---

## Chapter Eleven: Pride

Notes and Observations

Of all the characters in the Bible who seem so repugnant to us, probably no one is more so than the self-righteous Pharisee in the parable of Jesus, who prayed, "God, I thank you that I am not like other men, extortioners, unjust, adulterers, or even like this tax collector" (Luke 18:11). But the irony is that even as we condemn him, we can easily fall into the same self-righteous attitude.

In this chapter, we are going to address the sin of pride — not pride in general, but certain expressions of it that are special temptations to believers. We are going to look at the pride of moral self-righteousness, the pride of correct doctrine, the pride of achievement, and the pride of an independent spirit. As I seek to address these subtle sins, I pray that I can do so without myself falling into the pride of a censorious spirit. So let me say at the outset that I am not free from pride, especially the kind that hides itself behind a cloak of trying to teach others. One of the problems with pride is that we can see it in others but not in ourselves. And I am quite mindful of Paul's words, "You then who teach others, do you not teach yourself?" (Romans 2:21). So please join me in asking God to reveal to each of us the pride that *He* sees in our lives. That this is a critical topic is seen in the fact that both James and Peter warn us, "God opposes the proud" (James 4:6; 1 Peter 5:5).

## MORAL SELF-RIGHTEOUSNESS

The pride of the Pharisee in Jesus' parable was what we can call moral self-righteousness. It expresses itself in a feeling of moral superiority with respect to other people. This type of pride is not limited to believers. It is found in the political and cultural realms among both liberals and conservatives. Anyone who believes, for example, that he holds the moral high ground in any area such as politics, economics, or environmental policy is likely indulging in moral self-righteousness. Sadly, however, it is very common among conservative, evangelical believers.

The sin of moral superiority and self-righteousness is so easy to fall into today, when society as a whole is openly committing or condoning such flagrant sins as immorality, easy divorce, a homosexual lifestyle, abortion, drunkenness, drug use, avarice, and other flagrant and scandalous sins. Because we don't commit those sins, we tend to feel morally superior and look with a certain amount of disdain or contempt on those who do. It's not that those sins I've mentioned are not serious sins that are tearing apart the moral fabric of our society. Indeed, they are serious, and I respect those Christian leaders of our day who raise a prophetic voice against them. But the sin we ourselves fall into is the sin of moral self-righteousness and a resultant spirit of contempt toward those who practice those sins. In fact, Jesus told the parable about the Pharisee "to some who trusted in themselves that they were righteous, and treated others with contempt" (Luke 18:9).

I venture that of all the subtle sins we will address in this book, the pride of moral superiority may be the most common, second only to the sin of ungodliness. But though it is so prevalent among us, it is difficult to recognize because we all practice it to some degree. In fact, we seem to get a perverse enjoyment out of discussing how awful society around us is becoming. When we engage in this kind of thinking or conversation, we are guilty of the pride of moral superiority.

How, then, can we guard against the sin of self-righteousness? First, by seeking an attitude of humility based on the truth that "there but for the grace of God go I." Though that statement has become something of a trite expression, it is indeed true for all of us. If we are morally upright, and especially if we are believers who seek to live morally upright lives, it is only because the grace of God has prevailed in us. No one is naturally morally upright. Rather, we all have to say with David, "Surely I was sinful at birth, sinful from the time my mother conceived me" (Psalm 51:5, NIV). Rather than feeling morally superior to those who practice the flagrant sins we condemn, we ought to feel deeply grateful that God by His grace has kept us from, or perhaps rescued us from, such a lifestyle.

Another means by which we can guard against self-righteous pride is by identifying ourselves before God with the sinful society we live in. After the Babylonian captivity, when many of the Jewish people had returned to the land of Judah, Ezra, a scribe skilled in the Law of Moses went back to teach his people God's law. The Scripture says of Ezra that he "had set his heart to study the Law of the LORD, and to do it and to teach his statutes and rules in Israel" (Ezra 7:10). Ezra was obviously a godly man who lived an exemplary life.

Yet on an occasion when he became aware of some of the deep sin among the people, he identified himself with their sin, even though he himself was not guilty. Consider his prayer as recorded in Ezra 9:6: "O my God, I am ashamed and blush to lift my face to you, my God, for our iniquities have risen higher than our heads, and our guilt has mounted up to the heavens." Note how he included himself in his confession of guilt: "our iniquities" and "our guilt." As we in our day see the increasing moral degradation of our society, we need to adopt the attitude of Ezra. As we do so, it will tend to keep us from self-righteous pride.

## PRIDE OF CORRECT DOCTRINE

Closely akin to moral pride is doctrinal pride, the assumption that whatever my doctrinal beliefs are, they are correct, and anyone who holds another belief is theologically inferior. Those of us who care about doctrine at all are susceptible to this form of pride. It doesn't matter if we are Arminians or Calvinists, whether we subscribe to Dispensational or Covenant theology, or perhaps have embraced some form of eclectic theology, we tend to think our doctrinal beliefs are the correct ones and look with some disdain on those whose beliefs are different from ours. And then to complete the spectrum of this type of pride, there are those who don't consider doctrine important and so look with disdain on those of us who do. In other words, this form of pride is a pride in our particular belief system, whatever that may be, and an attitude that in our beliefs we are spiritually superior to those who hold other beliefs.

In 1 Corinthians 8, Paul addresses this form of pride when it arose over the issue of eating food that had been offered to idols. Some of the Corinthian Christians had concluded that such a practice fell within the bounds of Christian liberty. Paul did not disagree with that conclusion, but he did rebuke them for the doctrinal pride that resulted from their belief. He wrote to them, "Now concerning food offered to idols: we know that 'all of us possess knowledge.' This 'knowledge' puffs up, but love builds up" (1 Corinthians 8:1). Paul agreed with their "knowledge"—that is, their doctrinal belief regarding eating food offered to idols—but he charges them with doctrinal pride. Their "knowledge" had puffed them up.

If your Calvinism or Arminianism or dispensationalism, or your view concerning the end times, or your disdain for all doctrinal beliefs causes you to feel doctrinally superior to those who hold other views, then you are probably guilty of the sin of doctrinal pride. I'm not suggesting that we should not seek to know the truths of Scripture and develop doctrinal convictions about what the Scriptures teach; I am saying that we should hold our convictions in humility, realizing that many godly and theologically capable people hold other convictions.

I was once asked to comment about a book that taught a system of sanctification with which I strongly disagree. In my letter, I wrote the following: "Please note that I am saying 'things with which I disagree,' not things wherein he [the author] is wrong. I may find out when I get to heaven that I am the one who was wrong."

Now, having written that, does it mean my convictions are less strong than before? Not at all. If anything, after having read the book, my convictions were stronger. But it does mean that I want to hold my convictions with humility and treat the author of the book with the same respect I would treat people whose doctrine of sanctification is the same as mine. (I realize that in using myself as an example of the humility we should practice, I can appear to be "proud of my humility." I trust such is not the case, and I know there are other occasions when I have not been as generous and respectful toward those with whom I disagree.)

But the point of this section is to point out the danger of doctrinal pride and to urge you to prayerfully consider if this is one of your "acceptable" sins. If you even think it might be, I suggest you memorize and pray over the "knowledge puffs up" verse, 1 Corinthians 8:1. Then seek to pinpoint more precise areas where you tend to be doctrinally proud, and ask God to enable you to hold your convictions with a genuine spirit of humility.

## PRIDE OF ACHIEVEMENT

The Scriptures teach that there is generally a cause-and-effect relationship between hard work and success in any endeavor, whether in academics, athletics, business, or profession. For example, Proverbs 13:4 says, "The soul of the sluggard craves and gets nothing, while the soul of the diligent is richly supplied." And Paul exhorted Timothy regarding his ministry, "Do your best to present yourself to God as one approved" (2 Timothy 2:15). And Paul himself went all out in his ministry (see 1 Corinthians 9:26-27; Philippians 3:12-14).

However, the Scriptures also teach that success in any endeavor is under the sovereign control of God (see 1 Samuel 2:7; Psalm 75:6-7; Haggai 1:5-6). As the 1 Samuel passage teaches, "The LORD makes poor and makes rich; he brings low and he exalts." Two students in the same major can both work diligently, yet one excels and gets top grades, while the other barely gets above average. Why the difference? God has given one more intellectual ability than the other or perhaps brought him into the world in a family that challenged and stimulated his intellectual growth. Whatever the cause, the ability to achieve or succeed in any endeavor ultimately comes from God.

We looked at Deuteronomy 8:17-18 in session 3 (chapter 8) when considering the subject of thankfulness. But the reason we are to give thanks for our successes is that it is God who gives us the power to succeed. There is no such thing as the "self-made man" — that is, the man (or woman) who has "pulled himself up by his own boot straps." From a human point of view, he may appear to have succeeded by sheer dint of tenacity and hard work. But who gave him that entrepreneurial spirit and business acumen that enabled him to succeed? It was God.

To the proud Corinthians, Paul wrote, "Who sees anything different in you? What do you have that you did not receive? If then you received it, why do you boast as if you did not receive it?" (1 Corinthians 4:7). So what do you have that you did not receive? Nothing. You have nothing that did not come to you as a gift from God. Our intellect, our natural skills and talents, our health, and our opportunities to succeed all come from God. We have nothing that will enable us to achieve success that we did not receive from God.

So why do we boast, either in an overtly proud fashion or in a more subtle way in which we want to be proud but don't want to appear to be? In both instances, it is because we have failed to acknowledge that success came from God. Sure, there was diligent effort involved, but who gave you the ability and the desire to succeed? And who blessed your efforts? Ultimately, all is from God.

To me, one of the more obnoxious people is the blustery sort of person who lets everyone know that the secret to his success in business or whatever is his hard work. You expect that from an unbeliever, but when it comes from a Christian, it really is offensive. And the rest of us who are more quietly spoken can be just as offensive to God if we talk about our success, or the success of our children, without any acknowledgment of the gracious blessing of God.

Like most families, my wife and I receive a lot of Christmas letters with family news from friends and acquaintances we have made over the years. Occasionally, one of the letters might say something like this: "Our son, John, graduated summa cum laude from [some prestigious university such as Harvard, Yale, Stanford, or MIT]." Now, there is nothing wrong with communicating this good news to family and friends. But stated in the above fashion, the letter conveys the idea, "Isn't our son smart!" with no acknowledgment that his intellectual ability came from God.

If we want to avoid the subtle sin of pride in the achievements of our children, we might say something like this: "Our son, John, graduated summa cum laude from [fill in prestigious university]. We deeply acknowledge that John's intellectual abilities come from God, and we are profoundly grateful to Him. We know that God does not choose to endow every child with the abilities He has given John. We have tried to instill this grateful attitude in John and to teach him that his academic abilities are a stewardship entrusted to him by God to be used to serve others and to glorify God."

I've no doubt that other parents receiving such a letter from friends would rejoice with John's parents in the blessing of God on him. But apart from such acknowledgment, many parents, right or wrong, will feel perhaps a bit of envy because their children are just average or have not done well at all. Now, I've used academic excellence for the purpose of illustrating the principle, but the same would be true if John were the All-American quarterback at some big-time football school. Or if John is now in the business world and has been promoted to vice president of a successful company.

So whether it's our own success or that of our children, and in whatever endeavor it may be, failure to acknowledge that the success has ultimately come from God tends to promote a pride of achievement that does not honor God. And this form of pride is sin — subtle sin to be sure, but still sin.

Another aspect of the pride of achievement is the inordinate desire for recognition. All of us appreciate commendation for a job well done or for many years of faithful service on the job or at church. But what is our attitude when we do a specific job well and don't receive recognition? Are we willing to labor in obscurity, doing our job as unto the Lord, or do we become disgruntled over the lack of recognition?

Two principles from Scripture will help us guard against a sinful desire for recognition. First, we should remember the words of Jesus in Luke 17:10, "So you also, when you have done all that you were commanded, say, 'We are unworthy servants; we have only done what was our duty.'" When we have done a job well or served faithfully over a long time, our attitude should be, "I have only done my duty."

Second, we should learn that all recognition, regardless of its immediate source, ultimately comes from God. It is God who puts down one and lifts up another (see Psalm 75:6-7). Putting these two principles together causes us to say, "All is of grace." I deserve nothing, and all I do receive, including recognition, is only of His grace. Therefore, if I don't receive it, I will not fret.

## AN INDEPENDENT SPIRIT

Before starting on this book, I sent a proposed list of "acceptable" sins to about fifteen people in Christian ministry and asked them to add to the list any I had overlooked. From two who minister to students and young adults, I received a suggestion that I include the pride of an independent spirit. This spirit expresses itself primarily in two areas: a resistance to authority, especially spiritual authority, and an unteachable attitude.

Often these two attitudes go hand in hand. When we are young, we tend to think we know everything. Or, as one friend expressed it, "We don't know how much we don't know." When I was young and single, I lived with two different families who had young children. I now remember with shame how I used to silently judge their child rearing. What pride! Young and single with absolutely no experience in rearing children, yet I thought I knew more than they did.

In The Navigators' ministry, we often encounter a similar attitude among new and inexperienced staff. These folks are usually assigned to an intern role, serving under the direction of an experienced staff person. Yet they often come with an attitude that they know more about the ministry than the person who is to train them. As a result, they often exhibit an unwillingness to submit to the authority or instruction of the more mature staff person.

The Bible, however, is quite clear on the issue of submitting to authority. Of several Scriptures we could look at, the one that speaks most clearly to the subject is Hebrews 13:17:

> Obey your leaders and submit to them, for they are keeping watch over your souls, as those who will have to give an account. Let them do this with joy and not with groaning, for that would be of no advantage to you.

The writer of Hebrews probably had in mind the spiritual authority of elders in a local church. However, the principle of submission and teachability applies in any situation where someone is under the tutelage or training of a more mature believer. And it is our pride of an independent spirit that makes us unteachable or unsubmissive.

I well remember the night I was first exposed to the teaching of Hebrews 13:17. I was a fairly new officer in the U.S. Navy at the time. I well understood the concept of submission to the authority structure aboard ship, and I had no doubt assumed the authority of teachers and professors during my years in school. But the idea of a spiritual authority to which I should submit was a new and radical idea to me. I am grateful that God exposed me to this principle when He did. It so happened that the very next night I came in contact with The Navigators' ministry, which stresses one-to-one discipling and mentoring. Because of this new idea of submission to spiritual authority, I was teachable and responded readily to the challenges of being discipled by another.

Resistance to spiritual authority and an unteachable spirit is not limited to students and young adults. I sometimes encounter this attitude in teaching the Bible to older adults. Often a response to something I am teaching is, "Well, I think thus and such." No appeal to Scripture is made; it is only the person's opinion. Yet in his or her mind, that opinion is authoritative. There is no willingness to grapple with the teaching of Scripture.

Yet the Bible strongly teaches the value of a teachable attitude. Proverbs, in particular, has a lot to say about the subject. Consider, for example, the following phrases from the first few chapters of Proverbs:

My son, if you receive my words and treasure up my commandments with you . . . (Proverbs 2:1)

My son, do not forget my teaching, but let your heart keep my commandments. (Proverbs 3:1)

Hear, O sons, a father's instruction, and be attentive, that you may gain insight. (Proverbs 4:1)

My son, be attentive to my wisdom; incline your ear to my understanding. (Proverbs 5:1)

My son, keep my words and treasure up my commandments with you. (Proverbs 7:1)

Although all these Scriptures are in the context of a father/ son relationship, they all express the principle of teachability: a willingness, even a desire, to learn from those more mature in the faith.

To give balance to this section, let me say that spiritual authority does not mean that someone has the authority to tell you whom to marry (or not marry) or where you are to work. It does mean that there should be someone who has your best interests at heart and can speak to those and similar issues with wise, biblical counsel. It means that there are those more mature than you who can help you grow up to become a mature Christian yourself, able to help others.

Now, let's go back to the first objective of this book, which is to help us identify the subtle sins in our lives. One thing that may strike you is that some of the practices I've identi- fied as sin in this chapter are usually not regarded as sin at all. That's because they are so common and so accepted among Christians that we don't think of them as sin. Or, even if we do agree they are sins, we may see them in other people but not in ourselves.

So I urge you to pray over this chapter, asking God to bring to your mind any tendencies of pride in these areas and then confessing them as sin. As you do so, remember God's promise in Isaiah 66:2: "This is the one to whom I will look: he who is humble and contrite in spirit and trembles at my word."

---

## Chapter Twelve: Selfishness

Recently I learned, to my dismay, that one of my theological heroes from a bygone era had "feet of clay" — that is, some notable character flaws. One of his friends and admirers once wrote of him, "With all his glaring faults he was the greatest man I have known." What were those glaring faults? Elsewhere, this same friend described him as heartless, selfish, and domineering.

What a warning this should be to all of us. We can be very learned in our theology or very upright in our morality and yet fail to display the gracious qualities of Christian character that Paul called the fruit of the Spirit (see Galatians 5:22-23). Or to say it in another way more in line with the subject of this book, we can be orthodox in our theology and circumspect in our morality and yet tolerate in our lives some of the subtle "acceptable" sins we are discussing in these sessions. I believe that all of us have "blind spots," character flaws, or subtle sins, that we are not aware of. I doubt my hero deliberately tried to be heartless, selfish, and domineering. Those were blind spots that had never been dealt with. May God help us to deal with our own blind spots, including selfishness, as they occur in us.

In studying the sin of selfishness, it is helpful to start with the obvious truth that we are born with a selfish nature. One has only to observe preschoolers playing together to see that. How many times does a mother say, "Billy, share your toys with Bobby" or "Bobby, you mustn't grab toys from Billy like that"? As Billy and Bobby grow older, they learn that such obvious acts of selfishness are socially unacceptable, so their selfish acts become more subtle, but the problem is still there. Even after we become Christians, we still have the flesh that wars against the Spirit, and one of its expressions is selfishness.

Selfishness is a difficult sin to expose because it is so easy to see in someone else but so difficult to recognize in ourselves. In addition, there are degrees of selfishness as well as degrees of subtlety in expressing it. One person's selfishness may be crass and obvious. Such a person usually doesn't care what others think about him. Most of us, however, do care about what others think, so our selfishness will likely be more delicate and refined.

Selfishness may express itself in many ways, but for purposes of looking at our "respectable" sins, I am going to address four areas of selfishness that may be observed in believers. The first is selfishness with our *interests*. Paul wrote in Philippians 2:4, "Let each of you look not only to his own interests, but also to the interests of others." In using the word *interests*, Paul was undoubtedly referring to the concerns and needs of other people, but I am going to use it in a narrow sense to mean subjects we are interested in.

What are our interests? At this stage of our lives, my wife and I are interested in our grandchildren. We like to talk about them and show pictures of them to our friends. The problem is that our friends like to do the same. So when we are with them, whose grandchildren will we talk about? The answer, of course, is both if we and our friends are sensitive to the interests of each other. But if one or both couples are not sensitive, then the conversation is apt to be one-sided, or else we find ourselves waiting for our turn to share instead of showing a genuine interest in the other couple's grandchildren.

Now, I've used a specific example of talking about our grandchildren only to illustrate the tendency to be so interested in our own affairs that we have little or no interest in the affairs of others. Our interests might include our work, our hobbies, or anything else. My wife is a quilter, so it's natural when she's with other women who quilt to talk about their latest projects.

Again, she needs to be (and fortunately is) genuinely interested in the other women's work and not just her own.

At this point in time, I'm trying to write this book. I'm very interested in it, so when someone asks me a typical question, "What are you writing about these days?" it is so easy to get carried away and spend an inordinate amount of time talking about my book. But the person who asked me the question has interests of his own. I need to be sensitive to ask the other person about subjects (work, hobbies, children) that will give him an opportunity to talk about his interests.

A good test of the degree of selfishness in our interests would be to reflect on the conversation after you have been with someone (or with another couple) and ask yourself how much time you spent talking about your interests compared to listening to the other person.

Now, this form of selfishness may seem so harmless that you question why I include it in this chapter. At worst it seems only rude and usually is considered merely unthoughtfulness but certainly not sin. But it is a symptom of self-centeredness. It indicates we are concerned mostly about ourselves. In 2 Timothy 3:1-5, Paul provides a list of really ugly sins that will be characteristic of the "last days" — that is, our present age. Included in this list is "lovers of self." Lover of self is a good description of a selfish person. This person is first of all self-centered. At its extreme, the self-centered person cares little for the interests, needs, or desires of others. He is interested in only himself, and his self-centered conversation reflects that.

A second area of selfishness is in regard to our *time*. Time is a precious commodity, and each of us has only a fixed amount in a day. One can grow financially wealthy so as to have discretionary money, but few people have discretionary time. We all are busy, so it's easy to become selfish with our time. A husband was overheard saying to his wife, "My time is always more important than yours." This is obviously selfishness, but all of us can express a similar attitude in more polite ways.

Whether we are men or women, young or old, we tend to guard our time for our own ends. A student asks her roommate for help with an assignment, but the roommate is busy studying for an exam. Will she give up precious time to help her roommate, or will she guard it for herself? Or will she take time to help but do so in a reluctant manner?

What about the first student? Is she acting selfishly to ask her roommate for help when she knows the roommate is busy studying for the exam? We can be selfish by inordinately guarding our time, and we can also be selfish in unduly imposing on another person's time. In either case, we are thinking mainly about ourselves and our needs.

Selfishness with one's time will frequently be observed in the home. Usually husband and wife, and to some extent children, will have certain responsibilities and duties. Oftentimes there is a reluctance to step outside one's normal responsibilities. "That's not my job," is a response a child may make when asked to do something that's not his usual duty. Adults will usually not be so direct, but the selfish person will rarely see the needs of others in the family and will feel no sense of compassion toward one who seems overwhelmed at the time. There is seldom any expression such as, "I'll take care of that for you." Yet the Scriptures say that we are to "bear one another's burdens, and so fulfill the law of Christ" (Galatians 6:2). Going beyond our normal duties to help someone else is one way we can bear each other's burdens.

A third area of selfishness is with our *money*. Surveys show that Americans, who live in the richest nation in all of history, give less than 2 percent of their income to charitable and religious causes. While we pride ourselves on our generosity following major disasters, the facts state that we Americans as a whole are selfish with our money and relatively indifferent to the physical and material needs of people less fortunate than us. And even our relief giving tends to be a response to the more dramatic events. There was a great outpouring of money

119

following the tsunami of 2004 off the coast of Indonesia but almost no response to the almost equally devastating earthquake of 2005 in Pakistan.

This is an especially crucial issue for believers. The apostle Paul wrote that we are to "rejoice with those who rejoice, weep with those who weep" (Romans 12:15). And the apostle John wrote, "If anyone has the world's goods and sees his brother in need, yet closes his heart against him, how does God's love abide in him?" (1 John 3:17). Taken together, these verses tell us that we are to cultivate hearts of compassion toward those in need and then put that compassion to work through our giving.

As has already been observed in an earlier session, every dollar we receive, even when earned by our work, is a gift from God. We are to be stewards of that money and not consume all or most of it on ourselves. To do so is to be selfish with our money, while ignoring the needs of others. (There is more on this subject in session 9, chapter 20.)

The fourth area of selfishness we will look at is the trait of *inconsiderateness*. This trait may be expressed in several ways. The inconsiderate person never thinks about the impact of his or her actions on others. The person who is always late and keeps others waiting is inconsiderate. The person who talks loudly on his cell phone to the disturbance of others nearby is selfishly inconsiderate. So is the teenager who leaves her mess on the kitchen counter for someone else to clean up. Any time we do not think about the impact of our actions on others, we are being selfishly inconsiderate. We are thinking only of ourselves.

We can also be inconsiderate of the feelings of others. Far too often, Christians are rude to waitresses and store clerks. Or, at the very least, we are indifferent to their feelings. Instead of being rude or indifferent, we can with no expenditure of energy brighten someone's day with a simple thank you. Just as we need to cultivate the habit of giving thanks to God, we also need to develop that habit with one another. And in the home, a simple "thank-you" toward other family members goes a long way.

The person whose attitude is "I just say what I think and let the chips fall where they may" is selfishly inconsiderate. This person is completely indifferent to the possible embarrassment, humiliation, and put-down feeling of others. He is concerned only with expressing his own opinion.

We are to look not only to our own interests but also to the interests of others. If we broaden the meaning of interests to mean, as I believe Paul did, the needs and concerns of other people, we can see that the *unselfish* person is always balancing his or her needs and concerns with the needs and concerns of others. By contrast, the selfish person not only is indifferent to the needs of others but actually expects them to meet his needs and desires. This form of selfishness is found in marriages where each spouse expects the other to meet his or her needs, instead of thinking of how they can serve each other.

The greatest example of unselfishness is the Lord Jesus Christ, who though He was rich, for our sake became poor so that by His poverty we might become rich (see 2 Corinthians 8:9). And Paul urges us to cultivate the same frame of mind (see Philippians 2:5). Apart from Christ, one of the most notable examples of both selfishness and unselfishness occurred during the time of the bubonic plague that reached Europe in 1348 and was responsible for the deaths of 30 to 40 percent of Europe's population. The plague spread so quickly that when one member of a family was infected, often the whole family died. Because of that, sometimes the entire rest of the family would quickly get out, leaving the sick one to die alone. Many priests cared for the sick and dying, and as a result, they too died. Other priests refused to help. It was said at that time that the best of the priests died and the worst of them lived.

Living unselfishly will likely not cost us our lives, but it will cost. It will cost time and money. It will cost becoming interested in the interests, concerns, and needs of others. And it will cost in learning to be considerate of the emotions and feelings of others.

Notes and Observations

A lot of selfishness is exhibited in the home among family members. Outside the home we are apt to be on our best behavior and act as we know we should (though there are plenty of people who are selfish wherever they are). But in the home we tend to put aside those artificial restraints that are not part of our true character. And since selfishness is so difficult to see in ourselves, it would be good to ask other family members to point out any tendencies toward selfishness they see in us. And we should do this without becoming defensive or retaliating by bringing up selfishness in the other person. And then we should genuinely repent of our various sins of selfishness and begin to pray that the Holy Spirit will enable us to deal with those selfish traits.

I said early in the chapter that selfishness is easy to see in someone else but so difficult to recognize in ourselves. I suspect all of us have tendencies toward selfishness in one form or another, because we all still have the sinful flesh waging war against our souls. So please don't disregard this chapter as not applying to you. Rather, I urge you to go back through it, putting yourself in situations similar to the ones I have used for illustration. Ask the Holy Spirit to show you evidences of selfishness in your own life, and let Him use your family members as His agents.

# Pride and Selfishness

## (Chapters 11 and 12)

## STUDY QUESTIONS

KEY VERSES: "Love is patient and kind; love does not envy or boast; it is not arrogant or rude. It does not insist on its own way." (1 Corinthians 13:4-5)

## GET FOCUSED

When we think of godly prayers, we certainly don't think of the self-righteous Pharisee's prayer in Luke 18:11: "God, I thank you that I am not like other men . . . or even like this tax collector." After all, the Bible emphasizes that God hates *sinful pride* and opposes proud people.

Ironically, each of us can develop a similar self-righteous attitude. It is often easy to see sinful pride in others but be blind to our own pride. That's why, in this session, we'll look at four expressions of pride that especially tempt believers: pride of moral self-righteousness, pride of correct doctrine, pride of achievement, and pride of an independent spirit.

*Selfishness*, the other "respectable" sin we'll explore, is also insidious and hard for us to recognize in ourselves. It crops up everywhere — even in the lives of theological heroes. We all have blind spots toward our selfishness. We are born with a sinful nature and are easily tempted to care more about our interests than those of other people. Though our selfishness may be crass and obvious, usually it is more delicate and refined because we care about what other people think. That's one reason we'll address not only selfish interests but also being inconsiderate and selfish with time and money.

Let's face our pride and selfishness, knowing that God will help us battle them and become more like Jesus.

THINK IT THROUGH
For Personal Study

## *I. Pride of Self-Righteousness*

1. What does Scripture say about sinful pride (see James 4:6; 1 Peter 5:5) and the dangers that even believing teachers face (see Romans 2:1-3,21)?

2. "The sin of moral superiority and self-righteousness is so easy to fall into today," Jerry writes, "when society as a whole is openly committing or condoning such flagrant sins as immorality, easy divorce, a homosexual lifestyle, abortion. . . . Because we don't commit those sins, we tend to feel morally superior and look with a certain amount of disdain or contempt on those who do."

   a. Why do you suppose it is that we can so easily drift into the pride of moral superiority and then develop a spirit of contempt toward those who practice those sins?

   b. To what kind of people did Jesus tell the parable about the self-righteous Pharisee? Why is this significant to us? (See Luke 18:9.)

3. Believers who care deeply about a particular belief system are susceptible to pride of correct doctrine — thinking that people who hold other beliefs are theologically or spiritually inferior. What did Paul say to prideful believers who concluded that eating food sacrificed to idols fell within the bounds of Christian liberty? (See 1 Corinthians 8:1.)

## II.  Pride of Achievement and Independence

1. Where does our ability to achieve or succeed come from? (See Genesis 45:4-8; 1 Samuel 2:7; Daniel 2:21; Haggai 1:5-6.)

2. Read 1 Corinthians 4:7. How relevant are Paul's words to us today? Why?

3. How does God feel about a proud heart? (See Psalm 101:5; Proverbs 16:5; 21:4.) How does He feel about our failure to acknowledge His gracious blessings?

4. Which biblical principles help us guard against a sinful desire for personal recognition? (See Luke 17:10; Psalm 75:6-7.)

5. What do Proverbs 2:1; 3:1; 4:1; 5:1; and 7:1 emphasize (in the context of a father-son relationship), and why are the principles of these verses relevant to the topic of prideful independence versus a teachable spirit?

### III. The Sin of Selfishness

1. What is the root of our selfishness? (See Genesis 3:1-6; Jeremiah 17:9; Hosea 6:7; Romans 7:17-20; 8:6-7; Galatians 5:16-17; Ephesians 2:3.)

2. Which phrase in 2 Timothy 3:1-2 describes a selfish person? Why is this so convicting?

3. Because time is precious, it's easy to be selfish with it. What do the following verses reveal about sharing our time with others? (See Acts 9:36; Romans 16:2; Galatians 5:13; 6:2; 1 Thessalonians 5:14; Hebrews 6:10; 1 Peter 4:10.)

4. In contrast to someone who is inconsiderate — not thinking about how what he or she says or does affects other people — what does God say about being considerate? (See Titus 3:1-2; James 3:17.)

## TALK IT OVER
## FOR GROUP DISCUSSION

1. Do you agree with the author that "there are degrees of selfishness as well as degrees of subtlety in expressing it"? Why or why not?

2. Have five group members each look up one of the following verses: Psalm 31:23; Jeremiah 50:31; Luke 1:51; Proverbs 8:13; and Proverbs 15:25. After each verse is read aloud, discuss together the passage's insight on how God feels about sinful pride.

3. Why does God hate sinful pride? How does it minimize His work in our lives?

4. Why is it sometimes difficult to focus on and listen to other people's interest areas rather than talking about our own? How do our selfish tendencies influence our conversations? Our activities? Our thoughts?

5. If we allow sinful pride and selfishness to take root in our lives, what consequences should we expect? (See 1 Corinthians 5:6.) Can you think of a time when you allowed this to happen? What did you experience as a result? How do you think other people felt about you?

6. Have three participants read aloud Romans 12:1-3; Philippians 2:3; and 1 Corinthians 13:4. After each verse, identify how God wants us to counter the sins of pride and selfishness.

## GROUP PRAYER

Together, thank God for His blessings and ask Him for help in recognizing and dealing with the sins of pride and selfishness.

✤ ✤

FOR NEXT TIME: Read *Respectable Sins*, chapters 13, 14, and 15, and then respond to the "Think It Through" questions for session 6.

### SELFISHNESS IS NOT LOVE

Love cares more for others than for self.
Love doesn't want what it doesn't have.
Love doesn't strut,
Doesn't have a swelled head,
Doesn't force itself on others,
Isn't always "me first,"
Doesn't fly off the handle,
Doesn't keep score of the sins of others,
Doesn't revel when others grovel.

1 Corinthians 13:4-6, MSG

## TAKE IT TO HEART
### *A PERSONAL-GROWTH JOURNAL*

### *Personal Reflection*

In which particular area(s) of your life do sinful expressions of pride and selfishness tend to surface (home, work, school, recreation, thoughts)?

Your conversations can reveal clues regarding pride and selfishness. As you converse with others, do you truly listen and empathize, or do you tend to shift the conversation to your own stories, interests, or achievements? Write down an example or two, followed by your thoughts on how God probably wanted you to behave.

What do your calendar and checkbook reveal about selfishness in your life?

Compare the sins of pride and selfishness to the fruit of the Spirit (see Galatians 5:22-23). What changes might you need to make, with the Holy Spirit's help?

### *Personal Action Point and Prayer*

After you've identified areas of sinful pride and selfishness that may have taken root in your life, confess them to God in prayer. Ask Him to make you less mindful of yourself and more mindful of the needs of others.

---

## PROGRESS REPORT

Since the last session, did you catch pride and selfishness at work in your life? What brought it to your attention? How did you respond?

Why do you think pride and selfishness may be difficult to detect in ourselves?

As a result of your study of the "respectable" sins, how might your view of sin be changing?

# Impatience, Irritability, and Anger

BEFORE GATHERING: Read the following portion of *Respectable Sins*. In the margins, record observations, illustrations, or questions that come to mind as you read. Then answer the "Think It Through" study questions that follow the reading.

---

## Chapter Thirteen: Impatience and Irritability

Notes and Observations

A pastor friend of mine was visiting in the home of a couple who were founding members of his church, a couple who were greatly respected and loved and who had consistently invested their lives in other people. At the time of this particular visit, the husband had terminal cancer and did, in fact, die a few months later.

In the course of his visit, the pastor asked the couple, "How are you doing spiritually?" With tears in her eyes, the wife responded, "We're doing well as far as the cancer is concerned. But what I can't handle is our sin. After all these years, and especially in this situation, you would think we wouldn't still hurt and wound each other, but we do. And this is what I can't handle. I can handle the cancer, but I can't handle my sinful flesh."

This sad but true story illustrates a reality that is all too common about our "respectable" sins. We tend to exhibit many of these sins most freely in the context of our own families. As I have indicated in an earlier session, we can put on our "Christian face" outside the home, but with our families, our true character often comes out. This is especially true in the two areas of sin we will look at in this chapter: impatience and irritability.

These two traits are closely related. Furthermore, both

131

words can be defined in slightly different ways depending on the context. So in this chapter, I am going to define impatience as a strong sense of annoyance at the (usually) unintentional faults and failures of others. This impatience is often expressed verbally in a way that tends to humiliate the person (or persons) who is the object of the impatience.

The key to understanding this type of impatience is that it is a response to the usually *unintentional* actions of others. Because of my hearing disability, I can often *hear* my wife speaking to me but can't *understand* what she is saying. This is the type of situation that can easily create annoyance on her part when I ask her to repeat what she has said. So she has had to learn to be patient, as opposed to being impatient, with me in these instances. (In case you are wondering, I have tried a hearing aid, but it does not help my particular type of deafness.)

On my part, I like to live life with a time margin. I like to start early enough that I can get to church, or the airport, or wherever we might be going, in an unhurried fashion. My wife, on the other hand, has an incredible ability to be ready to go just in the nick of time. (How she times it this closely is a mystery to me.) So here I am ready to go but waiting on her. How will I handle this? Will I be impatient and say something such as, "Why are you always late?" or even say nothing but communicate my displeasure by my unspoken attitude of impatience? Or will I be patient with her, realizing that a harmonious relationship with her is more important than leaving the house at my prescribed time?

These real-life situations are only two examples of the frequent occasions where people living or working closely together have to continually guard against the temptation to become impatient. Because of our sinful flesh, we never "arrive" in the virtue of patience. All of us, including my wife and myself, are still in process.

Further, we should note that neither my hearing disability nor my wife's close timing causes either of us to be impatient.

They merely provide an opportunity for the flesh to assert itself. The actual cause of our impatience lies within our own hearts, in our own attitude of insisting that others around us conform to our expectations.

Can you identify recurring situations in your life that tempt you to become impatient? I hope you don't think, *Me? I don't have a problem with impatience.* You may not have a problem, but are you ever impatient? Let me suggest a few possibilities.

Parents can become impatient over the slow response to the training of children and teenagers. "How many times have I told you not to leave your shoes in the family room?" Or, "When are you going to learn to chew your food with your mouth closed?" These kinds of slow response to our training can often lead us to be impatient. Obviously the type of impatient expressions I've used as illustrations do not further our training efforts. They serve only to vent our impatience and humiliate the child. Family siblings are often impatient with one another, and it is a great challenge to parents to train their children, both by teaching and example, to be patient with others.

Though I have said we tend to exhibit impatience within our families, it is certainly not limited to that context. Some Christians are notorious for being impatient drivers. We can become impatient at the slowness of service in a store, at the bank, or in a restaurant. I have to guard against impatience at the post office when I only want to buy some stamps, but someone in line ahead of me has ten overseas packages to mail. You might want to ask your spouse, your teenagers, a friend who knows you well to help you identify areas of impatience in your life. Above all, we need to acknowledge and repent of our impatience as sin.

The apostle Paul, in several of his letters, exhorts us to be patient. In 1 Corinthians 13, the great "love" chapter, he leads off his description of love by saying, "Love is patient." In Galatians 5:22-23, patience is one of the nine expressions of the fruit of the Spirit. In Ephesians 4:1-2, Paul urges us to live our lives with patience, and in Colossians 3:12, we are to put on patience. Clearly, with Paul (who, I remind us, was not expressing merely his own opinion but was writing under the guidance of the Holy Spirit) the quality of patience is a virtue to be cultivated. And by reasonable inference we can say that impatience, the opposite of patience, is a sin to be put to death in our lives. Though it may be acceptable to us, it is not acceptable to God.

Now, I have said that impatience and irritability are closely related. While impatience is a strong sense of annoyance or exasperation, *irritability*, as I define it, describes the frequency of impatience, or the ease with which a person can become impatient over the slightest provocation. The person who easily and frequently becomes impatient is an irritable person. Most of us can become impatient at times, but the irritable person is impatient most of the time. The irritable person is one whom you feel you have to tiptoe or "walk on eggshells" around. This person is no fun to be with, but unfortunately family members or coworkers sometimes have no choice.

Are you upset with someone or some circumstance a lot of the time? If so, you may well be an irritable person. If you are frequently upset with another person (or persons), you may need to learn to overlook their unintentional actions. Proverbs 19:11, though addressing the topic of anger (our next chapter) says, "It is [one's] glory to overlook an offense." And Peter wrote, "Love covers a multitude of sins" (1 Peter 4:8). We might say that if love covers a multitude of sins, how much more should it cover a multitude of acts that irritate us.

Now, suppose you are someone who is frequently the object of another person's impatience. Suppose you are often berated, criticized, or chewed out. How should you respond? All too often a person of an equally strong temperament will respond in kind, thus starting a "war of words."[1] This approach is not only nonproductive, it is totally unbiblical.

Or you may be the type of person who doesn't respond verbally at all but inwardly seethes and resents the person who has vented his or her impatience at you. This is also a sinful response on your part.

Biblically you have two options. You can follow the example of Jesus, who, "when he was reviled, he did not revile in return; when he suffered, he did not threaten, but continued entrusting himself to him who judges justly" (1 Peter 2:23). Sometimes this may be your only biblical option.

The second option is to confront the person who is continually impatient toward you and point out to the person examples of his or her impatience. But this should be done only when you have resolved the issue in your own heart and can speak to the other person for his or her benefit, not just to make your own life more pleasant. If you have done this in a biblical manner and the person accepts what you say, you have likely enhanced your relationship with one another (see Matthew 18:15).

If the person is in denial about his or her impatience and becomes defensive or hostile when you point it out, then you should revert to the first option to follow the example of Jesus. To do this, however, requires a firm belief in the sovereignty of God in every situation of your life. God is likely using this person's sinful actions to help you grow in the biblical virtues of patience and meekness (see the example of Moses in Numbers 12:1-3).

Now, let me remind you, as I do in almost all the sessions, that this is a book about our "respectable" sins, the sins we tolerate in our lives while we condemn the more flagrant sins of society around us. May we be as severe with ourselves over our own subtle sins as we are with the vile sins we condemn in others. May we not be like the self-righteous Pharisee in the temple who prayed, "God, I thank you that I am not like other men" but may we continually have the humble attitude of the tax collector who said, "God, be merciful to me, a sinner" (Luke 18:11-13).

## Chapter Fourteen: Anger

Robert Jones, in his book *Uprooting Anger*, wrote, "Anger is a universal problem, prevalent in every culture, experienced by every generation. No one is isolated from its presence or immune from its poison. It permeates each person and spoils our most intimate relationships. Anger is a given part of our fallen human fabric." And then Jones added, "Sadly this is true even in our Christian homes and churches."[2]

I would add to Jones' observation about our Christian homes and churches that our anger is *often* directed toward those we should love most: our spouse, children, parents, or siblings in our human families, and those who are our true brothers and sisters in Christ in our church families. I once knew a fellow believer who was the epitome of graciousness to other people but was continually angry with his wife and children. Fortunately, after years of this, God finally convicted him and helped him deal with his anger.

What is anger? Many of us might say, "I can't define it, but I know it when I see it, especially if it's directed toward me." My dictionary defines anger simply as a strong feeling of displeasure, and usually of antagonism. I would add that it's often accompanied by sinful emotions, words, and actions hurtful to those who are the objects of our anger.

Anger is a huge and complex issue, and dealing with it extensively is beyond the purpose of this book. In keeping with my objective to help us confront the sins we tolerate in our lives, I am going to focus on that aspect of anger that we unconsciously treat as "acceptable" sin. In order to do that, I need to right away deal with the issue of righteous anger.

Some people justify their anger as righteous anger. They feel they have a right to be angry, given a certain situation. How, then, can I know if my anger is righteous anger? First, righteous anger arises from an accurate perception of true evil — that is, as a violation of God's moral law. It focuses on God and His will, not on me and my will. Second, righteous anger is always self-controlled. It never causes one to lose his temper or retaliate in some vengeful way.[3]

Though the Bible does give some examples of righteous anger, such as Jesus' cleansing of the temple, they are few. The main focus of the Bible's teaching on anger deals with our sinful anger, our sinful reactions to other people's actions or words. The fact that we may be reacting to another person's real sin does not necessarily make our anger righteous. We are likely more concerned with the negative impact of the sinful actions on us than we are that it is a violation of God's law. Or we may even use the fact that it is a violation of God's law to justify our own sinful angry response.

Another topic of anger that is also beyond the purpose of this book is that of the person who is continually angry, or the person whose anger causes him or her to be verbally or physically abusive. These people need good biblical and pastoral counseling. So in this chapter, I want to keep us focused on what we might call ordinary anger that we sort of accept as part of our lives but that is actually sinful in the sight of God.

In facing up to our anger, we need to realize that no one else *causes* us to be angry. Someone else's words or actions may become the occasion of our anger, but the cause lies deep within us — usually our pride, or selfishness, or desire to control. I agreed to do something for a friend, and then I forgot. When my failure came to light, he became quite angry with me. Why did he become so visibly upset? It was because my failure had made him look bad in front of some of his friends. This is not to excuse my forgetfulness and the real fact that I had put him in an awkward situation. But the cause of his anger was not my failure but his pride.

We may become angry because someone has mistreated us in some way. A person gossips about us, and when we hear about it, we get angry. Why? It's likely because our reputation or our character has been questioned. Again the cause is our pride.

We get angry because we don't get our way. We frequently see this in children, but it is just as true of us who are adults. Often in a marriage, either the husband or wife will have the stronger personality and will want to call the shots in the home, even at the expense of the other's desires or good judgment. When that person doesn't easily get his or her way, he or she tends to become angry.[4] Sometimes a similar situation occurs in a local church or even a parachurch ministry. A strong and often opinionated person again wants to exercise control and gets angry when others oppose him. In all of these instances, the cause of the anger is selfishness. "I want it *my* way."

We get angry as a response to someone else's anger. A husband comes home expecting dinner to be on the table. When it's not, he becomes angry and verbalizes his anger in hot and hurtful words. The wife gets angry in return, but she may not verbalize her anger. Instead she seethes inwardly with resentment. Her anger is just as sinful as her husband's. A man is chewed out by his boss, possibly in front of fellow employees. He can't retaliate in kind, but he, like the unfortunate wife, will also seethe with resentment.

These hypothetical situations are not intended to justify the actions of the husband or the boss. Clearly they are sinful. But we can choose how we will respond to the sinful actions of others toward us. Consider Peter's words to slaves in the first-century churches, who often served under cruel and unjust masters. According to much present-day thinking they would be justified in their anger, but here are Peter's words to them:

> Servants, be subject to your masters with all respect, not only to the good and gentle but also to the unjust. For this is a gracious thing, when, mindful of God, one endures sorrows while suffering unjustly. For what credit is it if, when you sin and are beaten for it, you endure? But if when you do good and suffer for it you

endure, this is a gracious thing in the sight of God.
(I Peter 2:18-20)

Peter's instructions to slaves are a specific application of a broader scriptural principle: We are to respond to any unjust treatment as "mindful of God." To be mindful of God means to think of God's will and God's glory. How would God have me respond in this situation? How can I best glorify God by my response? Do I believe that this difficult situation or this unjust treatment is under the sovereign control of God and that in His infinite wisdom and goodness He is using these difficult circumstances to conform me more to the likeness of Christ? (see Romans 8:28; Hebrews 12:4-11).

I am realistic enough to know that in the emotional heat of a tense situation, we are not going to go through a checklist of questions such as are in the preceding paragraph. But we can and should develop the habit of thinking this way. Oftentimes our immediate response to an unjust action of someone else will be sinful anger. This is certainly true of me. But in the after moments of a difficult episode, we can choose to continue to hold on to our anger, or we can reflect on such questions as I have given and allow the Holy Spirit to dissolve our anger.

I've no doubt there are myriad other circumstances or actions of other people that tempt us to be angry. But they can never *cause* us to be angry. The cause always lies within our hearts, usually as a result of our pride or selfishness.

There are probably exceptions to this that prove the rule, but apart from those, it is safe to say that all of us get angry from time to time. The issue is how we handle it. Some people tend to externalize their anger in strong, usually hurtful language. Others will externalize it in more subtle ways, such as belittling or making sarcastic comments to or about the person who is the object of their anger. And then there is the third group, who tend to internalize their anger in the form of resentment. All of these expressions of anger are sin.

So how should we handle our anger in a God-honoring way? First, we have to *recognize* and *acknowledge* our anger and the sinfulness of it. We cannot deal with anger until we acknowledge its presence. Then we need to ask ourselves why we became angry. Was it because of our pride or selfishness or some idol of the heart we are protecting? If so, we need to repent not only of our anger but also of our pride, selfishness, and idolatry.

Having to some extent dealt with the expression of our anger through recognition and repentance, we need to change our attitude toward the person or persons whose words or actions triggered our anger. Here the words of Scripture from Paul's pen should be our guide:

> Be kind to one another, tenderhearted, forgiving one another, as God in Christ forgave you. (Ephesians 4:32)

And again from Paul:

> . . . bearing with one another and, if one has a complaint against another, forgiving each other; as the Lord has forgiven you, so you also must forgive. (Colossians 3:13)

If we have expressed our anger outwardly, we also need to seek the forgiveness of the person we have wounded by our anger.

Finally, we need to hand over to God the occasion of our anger. This is especially true when we find ourselves the objects of someone else's anger or the objects of unjust treatment by a boss, an overbearing husband, or anyone who treats us unjustly or unfairly. To dissolve our sinful emotions, we must believe that God is absolutely sovereign in all the affairs of our lives (both the "good" and the "bad") and that all the words and actions of other people that tempt us to anger are somehow included in His wise and good purposes to make us more like Jesus. We must realize that any given situation that tempts us to anger can drive us either to sinful anger or to Christ and His sanctifying power.

Earlier in this chapter, I acknowledged that the subject of anger is complex and that addressing it significantly is beyond the purpose of this book. But I hope I have helped us to realize that most of our anger truly is sinful and, though we may excuse it and tolerate it in our lives, it is not acceptable to God. Before leaving this subject there is one more facet of anger we need to consider. That is the subject of . . .

## ANGER TOWARD GOD

I have encountered a number of Christians who are angry at God for some reason. Some of them think that God has let them down in some way; others feel that God is actually against them. I sit here now looking at a letter in which the writer says, "I have felt so many times that He has slapped me in the face when I was really depending on Him." This person freely admitted to being angry at God, because she had concluded that God was actually against her.

What are we to say to people who are desperately hurting and feel that God has let them down or is even against them? Is it okay to be angry toward God? Most pop psychology would answer yes. "Just vent your feelings toward God." I've even read the statement, "It's okay to be angry at God. He's a big boy. He can handle it." In my judgment, that is sheer blasphemy.

Let me make a statement loud and clear. It is *never* okay to be angry at God. Anger is a moral judgment, and in the case of God, it accuses Him of wrongdoing. It accuses God of sinning against us by neglecting us or in some way treating us unfairly. It also is often a response to our thinking that God owes us a better deal in life than we are getting. As a result, we put God in the dock of our own courtroom. I think of a man who, as his mother was dying of cancer, said, "After all she's done for God, this is the thanks she gets." Never mind that Jesus suffered untold agony to pay for her sins so she would not spend eternity in hell, this man thought that God also owed her a better life on this earth.

141

Notes and Observations

I acknowledge that believers can and do have momentary flashes of anger at God. I have experienced this myself. But we should quickly recognize those occurrences as the sins that they are and repent of them.

How, then, can we deal with our temptation to be angry at God? Must we just "stuff" our feelings and live in some degree of alienation from God? No, that is not the biblical solution. The answer lies, first of all, as I have said before (see session 4, chapter 9), in a well-grounded trust in the sovereignty, wisdom, and love of God. Second, we should bring our confusion and perplexity to God in a humble, trusting way. We can pray somewhat in the following fashion:

> God, I know that You love me, and I also know that Your ways are often beyond my understanding. I admit I am confused at this time because I do not see the evidence of Your love toward me. Help me, by the power of Your Spirit, to trust You and not give in to the temptation to be angry at You.[5]

Remember also that our God is a forgiving God. Even our anger toward Him, which I consider a grievous sin, was paid for by Christ in His death on the cross. So if you have anger in your heart toward God, I invite you — no, I urge you — to come to Him in repentance and experience the cleansing power of Christ's blood, shed on the cross for you.

I believe that many Christians live in denial about their anger. They consciously experience the flare-up of negative thoughts and emotions toward someone who has displeased them, but they do not identify this as anger, especially as sinful anger. They focus on the other person's wrongdoing and justify their own reaction. They do not see their sin. Consequently, their anger is "acceptable" to them. They sense no need to deal with it. I pray that God will be pleased to use this chapter to help all of us, whether our anger is occasional or frequent, recognize it as the sin that it is and take appropriate steps to deal with it.

---

## Chapter Fifteen: The Weeds of Anger

For reasons I will explain in a moment, we need to look more deeply at the topic of anger and anger's unruly offspring. We tend to think of our anger in terms of episodes. We get angry, and then we get over it. Sometimes we apologize to the person who is the object of our anger, and sometimes we don't. But somehow the other person, apology or not, gets over his defensive response, whether an angry outward retort or an inner resentment, and life goes on as usual. The relationship has been scarred but not broken. It's not a great way to live with one another, but it's tolerable. That seems to be the way far too many believers view the sin of anger. They've just come to accept it as part of life.

The Bible, however, is not so sanguine about our anger. Rather, it tells us to put it away (see Ephesians 4:31; Colossians 3:8). If you take the time to look up these texts, you will see that in each of them, anger is associated with such ugly sins as bitterness, clamor, wrath, slander, malice, and obscene talk. It is also included in a similar list of despicable sins in 2 Corinthians 12:20. Clearly, anger does not keep good company. It often associates itself with what we would consider more serious sins and actually leads to some of them.

But what about the Scripture that says, "Be angry and do not sin; do not let the sun go down on your anger" (Ephesians 4:26)? Paul is not granting permission to be angry, let alone commanding it, as the imperative mood might suggest. Rather, Paul takes it for granted that we will become angry, and he is telling us how to handle it. Basically he is saying, "Don't hold on to your anger. Get over it quickly." That's why he adds the clarifying statement, "Do not let the sun go down on your anger."

We have an idiomatic expression, "Nip it in the bud." That's what Paul is telling us to do. Deal with your anger swiftly, but above all, don't go to bed with it still in your heart. At best, anger is sin (with the rare exception of true righteous anger), and at worst, it leads to even greater sins.

In this chapter, we are going to look at some of the long-term results of anger; what I call "weeds of anger." I have deliberately chosen the word *weeds* because weeds are always something we want to get rid of. But the weeds of anger are not benign; they are noxious. They can poison our minds and the minds of others around us. What, then, are some of the noxious weeds that spring up from unresolved anger?

*Resentment* is anger held on to. Most often it is internalized. It arises in the heart of a person who is ill-treated in some way but who does not feel in a position to do anything about it. An employee may feel ill-treated by his boss but doesn't dare react in an outwardly angry fashion, so he internalizes it in the form of resentment. A wife may react similarly toward an overbearing husband. Resentment may be more difficult to deal with than outwardly expressed anger because the person often continues to nurse his wounds and dwell on his ill-treatment.

*Bitterness* is resentment that has grown into a feeling of ongoing animosity. Whereas resentment may dissipate over time, bitterness continues to grow and fester, developing an even higher degree of ill will. It is usually the long-term reaction to real or perceived wrong when the initial anger is not dealt with.

An elder intervened in a situation regarding a teenage girl in his local church. The girl's father thought the elder had mishandled the situation. Instead of seeking to resolve the issue, he became angry and then bitter. In the words of the pastor, he was "eaten up with bitterness." The father said to the pastor, "I've forgiven him, but I don't want anything to do with him." Quite obviously he had not forgiven. True forgiveness results in a restored relationship, not continuing animosity. This man was consumed with bitterness, but in his self-righteousness he couldn't see it. All he could see was the perceived or actual wrong of the elder, which he continued to dwell on.

As this story illustrates, bitterness frequently occurs within a local church family. Someone is ill-treated in some way, or at least she thinks she has been. Instead of seeking to resolve the issue, she allows her hurt to fester and over time becomes bitter. Or it may be that she has sought to resolve the issue and the other person does not respond. Perhaps she has even gone to one of the pastoral staff who doesn't seriously listen to her and so dismisses her with the thought that it is all her problem. But regardless of the actual or perceived ill-treatment, bitterness is never a biblical option. We can be hurt, and acknowledge that we have been hurt, without becoming bitter.

Of course, bitterness can occur in any interpersonal relationship, but it too often occurs among people who should love each other. I referred to the church *family*. That's what we are. We are brothers and sisters in Christ. But bitterness may also occur in human families among physical brothers and sisters. A son or daughter may feel that the parents are showing favoritism toward a sibling, and, in fact, that might be an accurate perception. But if the son or daughter is a Christian, he or she must not nurse that feeling until resentment becomes bitterness. Sometimes adult siblings can become bitter over failing to receive what they consider their fair share of the family inheritance. Once again, for the person who wants to follow Christ, bitterness is never an option.[6]

*Enmity* and *hostility* are essentially synonymous and denote a higher level of ill will or animosity than does bitterness. Whereas bitterness may to some degree be marked by polite behavior, enmity or hostility is usually expressed openly. Often it is in the form of denigrating or even hateful speech toward or about the objects of the animosity. Additionally, though bitterness may be harbored within one's own heart, enmity or hostility usually

145

spreads its poison outward to involve other people.

*Grudge* (as in holding a grudge) occurs five times in the Bible (see Genesis 27:41; 50:15; Leviticus 19:18; Psalm 55:3; Mark 6:19). It will help us understand the depths of animosity and ill will implied in the word *grudge* when we see that in the two Genesis texts, the English Standard Version uses *hate* instead of *grudge*. In all five occurrences, the word is associated with taking revenge on the object of the grudge. For example, Esau *hated* Jacob and planned to kill him (see Genesis 27:41). Joseph's brothers were afraid he would *hate* them and pay them back for all the evil they had done to him (see Genesis 50:15). In the New Testament, Herodius had a *grudge* against John the Baptist and wanted to put him to death (see Mark 6:19).

Today we probably wouldn't associate holding a grudge with plans to kill someone. Oftentimes, however, people will plan, if only in their minds, ways to get revenge against the person they hold a grudge against. They usually dare not execute those plans, but they get a perverse enjoyment out of going over them in their minds. This can be true even among Christians. That is why Paul found it necessary to write the exhortation of Romans 12:19-21:

> Beloved, never avenge yourselves, but leave it to the wrath of God, for it is written, "Vengeance is mine, I will repay, says the Lord." To the contrary, "if your enemy is hungry, feed him; if he is thirsty, give him something to drink; for by so doing you will heap burning coals on his head." Do not be overcome by evil, but overcome evil with good.

*Strife* describes open conflict or turmoil between parties, usually between opposing groups as distinct from individuals. That's why we speak of "church fights" or "family feuds." It's always ugly and goes beyond the bounds of "respectable" sins, and it certainly isn't subtle. But I include it because it often occurs between self-righteous Christians who never consider the possibility that their own attitudes or heated words contribute to the strife. In their minds, it is always the other party who is in the wrong and is causing the strife.

The above descriptions of these noxious "weeds of anger" are not intended to be dictionary definitions of terms, nor do I mean to draw a sharp distinction between them. Terminology here is not important. What I want us to see is that anger, held on to, is not only sin, it is spiritually dangerous. And if you will scan back over these weeds, you will see that there is something of an escalation of feelings of ill will and dissension. Anger is never static. If it is not dealt with, it will grow into bitterness, hostility, and revenge-minded grudges. No wonder that Paul said, "Do not let the sun go down on your anger."

How, then, can we deal with our anger so that it does not begin to sprout these noxious weeds? How can we nip it in the bud so that the sun does not go down on it? Let me give three basic directions.

First, we must always look to the sovereignty of God. God doesn't cause people to sin against us, but He does allow it, and it is always allowed for a purpose — most often our own growth in Christlikeness. When Joseph was grievously sinned against by his own brothers and sold into slavery, he did not become bitter. Instead he could say to his brothers, "It was not you who sent me here, but God" (Genesis 45:8). Granted, he said those words after he had been elevated to the second highest position in Egypt, but they were true from the day the brothers sold Joseph into slavery. And during those years as a slave in Potiphar's house and the subsequent years as a prisoner for a crime he did not commit, the biblical narrative never suggests that Joseph became bitter. Instead it tells us that he did his work well (certainly not the attitude of a bitter person) and was so well regarded by Potiphar and the keeper of the prison that both of them put him in charge of major responsibilities.

I have found that a firm belief in the sovereignty of God is my first defense against a temptation to allow anger to linger in my mind and emotions. If I want to deal with the temptation decisively, I actively call to my mind that the actions of another person (or persons) that triggered my initial response of anger are under the sovereign control of God. Though the actions may be sinful in themselves, God intends them for my good. As Joseph said to his brothers, "As for you, you meant evil against me, but God meant it for good" (Genesis 50:20).

As I have already observed, the good may be an opportunity to grow in Christlikeness. But God may also have other ends in view, perhaps to prepare us in some way for greater usefulness. Or we may never know what good God brought out of a specific situation where we were tempted to become angry. But it is enough to know that however difficult the situation, and however strong the resultant temptation to become angry, God intends good. Actively reflecting on this great truth of God's sovereignty is my first step to defuse anger.

Second, we should pray that God will enable us to grow in love. In 1 Peter, which is a letter urging its readers to pursue holiness, even in the face of tough times, Peter keeps emphasizing the importance of brotherly love — that is love toward fellow believers. For example, he writes, "Above all, keep loving one another earnestly, since love covers a multitude of sins" (1 Peter 4:8).

Peter's words mean that love enables us to overlook a lot of sinful actions of other people. If someone snubs you or does something that embarrasses you or inconveniences you, love will enable you to overlook it. Remember, we can choose how we react to the real or perceived wrong actions of other people. The phrase I've already used twice in this chapter, "nip it in the bud," especially applies here. While love may not "cover" significant sins against us, it can certainly cover many ordinary wrongs.

When the strong-willed husband comes home and finds the house in a mess and dinner not prepared, he can allow love to cover the situation. In fact, if he follows the path of love, he will not only overlook that which tempts him to anger, he will roll up his sleeves and pitch in to help. He will follow the example of the Lord Jesus, who in full awareness of His deity performed the most menial task of washing the disciples' feet (see John 13:2-15).

We are to love one another *earnestly*; that is, we are to pursue it diligently. The love that overlooks an offense doesn't just happen. It comes as we pursue it diligently in dependence on the Holy Spirit.

The apostle Paul echoes Peter's words when he writes, "[Love] . . . is not easily angered" (1 Corinthians 13:5, NIV). That is a statement we all need to ponder. Are you easily angered? Can just a little sarcastic remark by someone almost ruin your day, or can you, out of love for the person who made the remark, shrug it off or "cover" it? There is probably nothing more corrosive in interpersonal relationships than an unruly tongue (see James 3:5-10). In session 7 (chapter 17), we'll address this issue from the standpoint of the speaker, but for now let's focus on our response toward someone else's tongue.

We're all familiar with the old rhyme, "Sticks and stones may break my bones, but words can never hurt me." And we all know it isn't true. Sinful words do hurt, especially if they come from someone close to us, but we can choose whether or not they make us angry. We can absorb the hurt as real hurt without becoming angry at the person who spoke the hurtful words. But to do that, we must love that person deeply so that we are not easily angered by unkind words.

Paul also tells us, "[Love] . . . keeps no record of wrongs" (1 Corinthians 13:5, NIV). Do you tend to file away in your mind wrongs done to you? This is a sure road to bitterness. The statement, "I can forgive, but I can't forget," simply isn't true. If you keep rehearsing in your mind old hurts that occurred months or maybe even years ago, you haven't forgiven. You are simply feeding your bitterness. To keep no record of wrongs means we cease to bring them up to ourselves or to another party. It does not mean we erase the hurt from our minds. We can't do that. But it does mean we don't actively keep bringing it up and feeding on it. And it also means that if it does come to our minds involuntarily, perhaps triggered by another incident, we immediately dismiss it. We do not give it a chance to gain a foothold in our conscious thinking.

The third direction is to learn to forgive as God has forgiven you. The Scripture that helps me most to practice forgiveness is the parable of the unforgiving servant (see Matthew 18:21-35). The occasion of the parable was Peter's question to Jesus, "Lord, how often will my brother sin against me, and I forgive him? As many as seven times?" (verse 21), which means, as often as he sins, however many times that is, is well known to us. Then Jesus tells the parable of the unforgiving servant. However, the parable doesn't speak directly to the number of times we are to forgive, but to the basis of our forgiving one another.

The parable tells of a king's servant who owed the king ten thousand talents. A talent was six thousand denarii. Without going into the math, the servant owed the equivalent of 200,000 years of wages for the typical laborer. That would be about six to eight billion dollars in our present-day labor market. Jesus sometimes used hyperbole to make His point, and this was one of those occasions. There was no way a servant to the king could have accumulated such a huge debt, but we'll see shortly why Jesus used such an immense sum of money.

The servant begged for patience on the part of the king to give him time to repay what he owed. This was purely wishful thinking on the servant's part. There was no way he could repay it. So the king took pity on him and forgave him the debt.

Then this servant went away from the king's presence and found a fellow servant who owed him one hundred denarii — about one-third of a year's wages or by today's reckoning about ten to fifteen thousand dollars. This second servant also pleaded for patience, but the servant who had just been forgiven of over six billion dollars refused and committed him to prison.

The message of the parable turns on the vast difference between the amounts of the two debts: over six billion dollars and ten to fifteen thousand dollars. Ten to fifteen thousand dollars is not an insignificant sum, even to us today. But for the disciples who heard this parable directly from Jesus, it would have been even more significant, a third of a year's wages.

Now, the first sum of money represents our moral and spiritual debt to God. Though in the master/servant world of that day, six to eight billion dollars would be hyperbole, in our relationship with God, it is an accurate representation of our debt to Him. Regardless of how moral and spiritual we have been, the debt of our sin is enormous. The damage to God's glory by our sin is determined not by the severity of our sin but by the value of God's glory.

If I spill black indelible ink on a rug you bought at the local discount store, that's bad. But if I spill the same ink on your very expensive Persian rug, that's really bad. Why? My act is the same and the ink is the same, but the value of the two rugs is vastly different. The extent of the damage is determined not by the size of the ink blobs on the two rugs but by the respective value of each of them.

This is how we should think of our sin against God. Every sin we commit, regardless of how insignificant it seems to us, is an assault on His infinite glory. And the value of an expensive rug, even if it's millions of dollars, is nothing compared to the value of God's glory. So we all are represented by the first servant who owed ten thousand talents. Our debt to God is utterly unpayable.

Let's go back to the parable. What happened to the billions of dollars the first servant owed? Could the king just walk away and forget it? Were there no financial consequences to him? No, it's not that easy. The moment the king forgave the debt, his net worth was reduced by six to eight billion dollars. It cost the king tremendously to forgive his servant's debt.

In the same manner, it cost God to forgive us. It cost Him the death of His Son. No price can be put on that death, but God paid it so He could forgive each of us of the enormous spiritual debt we owed to Him.

The message should be clear. The moral debt of wrongdoing, of sinful words and acts against us, is virtually nothing compared to our debt to God. I'm not minimizing the seriousness of hurts or damages you may have experienced. In the parable, ten to fifteen thousand dollars was a lot more than coffee-break money at work. It was a third of a year's wages. And the wrongs you have suffered may be much more than an occasional snub or word of gossip about you. They may have been quite damaging to you in some way. But compared to the damage each of us has done to God's glory, it's a small amount.

This basis of our forgiving one another, then, is the enormity of God's forgiveness of us. We are to forgive because we have been forgiven so much. Until we acknowledge that we are the ten-thousand-talent debtor to God, we will struggle with forgiving people who have wronged us in significant ways or people who continue to wrong us.

But once we embrace the reality that we truly are such debtors to God because of our *continual* sin against Him, we can say when wronged, "God, that was a terrible wrong against me, but I am the ten-thousand-talent debtor. His sin against me was nothing compared to my sin against You, and because You have forgiven me, I, from my heart, forgive that person."

I don't want to imply that praying in such a way, even when done sincerely, will cause our anger to immediately disappear. The flesh doesn't give up that easily. But the attitude expressed in such a prayer does give us a weapon to use to put our anger to death.

As we come to the end of this second chapter on anger, I'm sure that both chapters raise some questions or objections. Some readers may think I'm ignoring such tough issues as abusive parents or spouse, or some of the systemic injustices prevalent in our society. Some may think, *He doesn't know what I've been through. If he did, he wouldn't be so smug with his answers.*

In response, let me say that it is beyond the purpose of this book to address the various issues that trigger our anger. And I certainly don't advocate that we play "doormat" Christianity, letting people continually run over us or abuse us. There are times when we must stand up for what is right and just. But we should not sin in the process. That is what I'm after.

My goal in these two chapters is to help us face the fact that much, if not most, of our anger is sinful, even though it may arise from the sinful actions of others. In emphasizing our sin of anger, I do not mean to minimize the sin of those other people. But there is an old saying, "Two wrongs never make a right." The other person's sin does not make our sin of anger "right" or justifiable. Or as James wrote, "The anger of man does not produce the righteousness that God requires" (1:20).

Furthermore, I suspect that much of our anger is not a result of significant injustices or wrongs against us but is the manifestation of our own pride and selfishness. I have been embarrassed or inconvenienced or frustrated by the actions (or even the inactions) of other people, so I get angry. While there is plenty of injustice that deserves a response of righteous anger, we should not use that as an excuse to evade the reality of the sinful anger that so often arises in our hearts and may be expressed by our words or actions.

So again, I commend to you the three principles or practices that I find so helpful: a firm belief in the sovereignty of God; a diligent pursuit of brotherly love that covers a multitude of sins and does not keep a record of wrongs; and a humble realization that, in comparison to my brother's sin against me, I am the ten-thousand-talent debtor to God.

# Impatience, Irritability, and Anger

## (Chapters 13, 14, and 15)

## STUDY QUESTIONS

KEY VERSES: "I . . . urge you to walk in a manner worthy of the calling to which you have been called, with all humility and gentleness, with patience. . . . I fear that perhaps when I come . . . there may be quarreling, jealousy, anger." (Ephesians 4:1-2; 2 Corinthians 12:20)

## GET FOCUSED

Jim and Susan arrived at the restaurant ten minutes apart. "Well, you're late as always," he quipped.

"I'd have been on time," she retorted, eyes flashing, "if you hadn't left the car almost out of gas again."

Moments later, each of them stormed out. *I'll go work out,* Jim thought, *then get fast food. He's some piece of work,* Susan muttered to herself. *He sleeps on the couch tonight.*

"Respectable" sins of impatience, irritability, and anger often surface among friends and family.

Impatience and irritability crop up easily, such as when we wait at the post office or a spouse or child consistently but unintentionally annoys us. It causes us to speak or behave in ways that hurt those we love and dishonor our Lord Jesus Christ.

Sinful anger can create even greater damage. We often ignore or deny this sin, so we'll focus on it a little more — and on its damaging offshoots, such as bitterness and strife.

According to Jerry Bridges, situations that arouse impatience, irritability, and anger can either drive us to sin or they can drive us to Christ and His sanctifying power. We must carefully determine ahead of time how we will respond when tempted to express impatience, irritability, and anger — and when people express them toward us. Will we vent our emotions with negative words, expressions, and body language? Or will we choose to trust in God's sovereignty, wisdom, and love? Big choices . . . with big consequences.

# THINK IT THROUGH
## FOR PERSONAL STUDY

### *I.  Impatience and Irritability*

1.  Jerry defines *impatience* as "a strong sense of annoyance at the (usually) unintentional faults and failures of others." In what ways do you tend to express impatience? How do these expressions affect those people who are objects of your impatience?

2.  Situations do not cause us to be impatient. "They merely provide," the author writes, "an opportunity for the flesh to assert itself. The actual cause of our impatience lies within our own hearts, in our own attitude of insisting that others around us conform to our expectations." Is Jerry's statement a new distinctive for you? Why is it important for us to understand this perspective?

3.  Speaking through Paul in the Scriptures below, how does God want us to act when we're tempted to be impatient?

   1 Corinthians 13:1,4:

   Galatians 5:22-23:

Ephesians 4:1-2:

4. *"Irritability,"* writes the author, "describes the frequency of impatience, or the ease with which a person can become impatient over the slightest provocation." Keeping Jerry's definition in mind, do you agree that irritability is a sin? What do you think lies at the root of the irritability? Be specific and explain your response.

## II. *Anger and Its "Weeds"*

1. Jerry defines anger as "a strong feeling of displeasure, and usually of antagonism . . . often accompanied by sinful emotions, words, and actions hurtful to those who are the objects of [the] anger." To what extent do you think anger has permeated our homes, friendships, and churches? Why?

2. Contrast what the Bible reveals about *righteous* anger with what it says about *sinful* anger:

a. Righteous anger (self-controlled, arises from an accurate perception of evil, focuses on God and His will):

Exodus 32:15-20:

Nehemiah 5:1-8:

Matthew 21:12-13:

b. Sinful anger (sinful reactions to people's actions and words):

Matthew 5:22:

Galatians 5:19-20:

Ephesians 4:29-31:

3. Read Ephesians 4:32 and Colossians 3:13. What guidance do these verses offer for guarding our attitude toward people whose words or actions tempt us to be impatient, irritable, and/or angry?

## TALK IT OVER
### FOR GROUP DISCUSSION

1. Do you agree with the author that circumstances or people's actions can never *cause* us to be impatient, irritable, or angry? Explain your answer.

2. Discuss this statement: "We can choose how we will respond to the sinful actions of others toward us." Do you agree or disagree? Why?

3. What are the *real* causes of impatience, irritability, and sinful anger? Once we recognize them, what practical steps can we take to deal with them:

　　a. *proactively* — before situations arise?

　　b. *responsively* — in the heat-of-the-moment situation?

　　c. *retrospectively* — once the Holy Spirit makes you aware that you've "blown it"?

4. Imagine that a good friend keeps justifying his or her sinful anger and refuses to face the deeper, causative issues. What might you say to him or her?

5. How has the sovereign God, in His wise and good purposes for you, used difficult situations (including impatient, irritable, and angry people) to teach you more about Him and the Christian life?

## GROUP PRAYER

Ask God to help each of you, through the guidance of the Holy Spirit, to deal with impatience, irritability, and anger *proactively*, *responsively*, and *retrospectively* in the coming week.

❧ ❧

FOR NEXT TIME: Read *Respectable Sins*, chapters 16 and 17. Then respond to the "Think It Through" personal-study questions for session 7.

---

### TAKE IT TO HEART
#### *A PERSONAL-GROWTH JOURNAL*

### *Personal Reflection*

Through your reading and study this week, what has God revealed to you about your tendencies to be impatient, irritable, or angry?

What commitment(s) are you willing to write down — right now — about how you intend to deal with these sins in the future? (Think proactively, responsively, and retrospectively.)

### *Personal Action Point and Prayer*

Write out your heart's prayer, asking God to help you, through His Holy Spirit, to keep your proactive, responsive, and retrospective commitments when dealing with these "respectable" sins.

---

# Battling Anger's "Noxious Weeds"

Long-term, unresolved anger creates many "noxious weeds" that poison lives. Use the following verses as a springboard to further explore the effects of these "weeds." Ask God to reveal any area in which He sees a weed growing in your life, and then recognize it and deal with it according to the guidance in the suggested Scripture references. If one or more of these conditions surfaces often — or in a way that leads to verbal or physical abuse of anyone — seek good Bible-based (pastoral) counseling.

Use the spaces below to note any personal tendencies God may be revealing to you. Summarize His message to you in the corresponding Scriptures.

RESENTMENT — internalized, unresolved anger that is held onto. *(See 1 Corinthians 13:5; 2 Timothy 2:22-24.)*

BITTERNESS — resentment that has grown into ongoing animosity. *(See Romans 3:12-14; James 3:14.)*

HOLDING A GRUDGE — taking revenge on the object of the grudge. *(See Romans 12:18-21; James 5:9.)*

STRIFE — open conflict or turmoil between people. *(See Proverbs 30:33; Romans 1:29; 1 Timothy 6:3-4.)*

BONUS STUDY

# Learning to Forgive

Read Jesus' parable of the unforgiving servant in Matthew 18:21-35. Then respond thoughtfully, in writing, to the following prompts:

From the parable, what can we learn about forgiving others as God has forgiven us?

Every sin we commit, regardless of how insignificant it seems to us, is an assault on God's infinite glory. What did it cost God to forgive us?

How should we then live?

How should we then forgive others?

## PROGRESS REPORT

Since the last session, when have impatience or anger surfaced in your life? In the lives of people around you? How did you respond?

What is at the root of irritability, and what impact does it have on those around us? Have you been more aware of it this week than before? Why or why not?

Together, review ways in which each of us can deal more effectively with such sins through the power of the Holy Spirit.

# Judgmentalism and Sins of the Tongue

Before Gathering: Read the following portion of *Respectable Sins*. In the margins, record observations, illustrations, or questions that come to mind as you read. Then answer the "Think It Through" study questions that follow the reading.

---

## Chapter Sixteen: Judgmentalism

Notes and Observations

The sin of judgmentalism is one of the most subtle of our "respectable" sins because it is often practiced under the guise of being zealous for what is right. It's obvious that within our conservative evangelical circles there are myriads of opinions on everything from theology to conduct to lifestyle and politics. Not only are there multiple opinions but we usually assume our opinion is correct. That's where our trouble with judgmentalism begins. We equate our opinions with truth.

Of course, judgmentalism is not limited to conservative evangelicals. It permeates our society and occurs on either side of the cultural divide. The animal rights activists who burn medical research clinics and the extreme environmentalists who vandalize ski slopes are acting out their judgmentalism. The person who says, "Jesus wouldn't drive an SUV," is judgmental, not because Jesus *would* drive an SUV (that's not the point) but because the person has made a dogmatic and judgmental statement based purely on personal opinion.

I grew up in the mid-twentieth century, when people dressed up to go to church. Men wore jackets and ties (usually suits and ties) and women wore dresses. Sometime in the 1970s, men began to show up at church wearing casual pants and open-collar shirts. Many women began to wear pants. For several years, I was judgmental toward them. *Didn't they have any reverence for God? Would they dress so casually if they were going to an audience with the president?* That sounded pretty convincing to me.

Only I was wrong. There is nothing in the Bible that tells us what we ought to wear to church. And as for dressing up to meet the president, that's a cultural thing centered in Washington, DC. If you were invited to meet the president while he is vacationing at his ranch, you would probably show up in blue jeans. Reverence for God, I finally concluded, is not a matter of dress; it's a matter of the heart. Jesus said that true worshipers are those who worship the Father in spirit and truth (see John 4:23). Now, it's true that casual dress may reflect a casual attitude toward God, but I cannot discern that. Therefore, I should avoid ascribing an attitude of irreverence based purely on a person's dress.

I also grew up in the era of the grand old hymns sung to the accompaniment of piano and organ. It was majestic. To me, it was reverent worship of God. Today, in many churches, the grand old hymns have been replaced by contemporary music, and the piano and organ with guitars and drums. Again, I was judgmental. *How could people worship God with those instruments?* But the New Testament churches had neither pianos nor organs, yet they managed to worship God in psalms, hymns, and spiritual songs (see Colossians 3:16). I still have a preference for church music sung as we did when I was younger, but it's just that — a preference — not a Bible-based conviction. It's true that a lot of contemporary music is shallow and human-centered. But there is much that is as God-honoring and worshipful as our traditional hymns. So let's avoid being judgmental.

We have convictions that we elevate to biblical truth on a number of issues. I wrote somewhere that I had finally come to the conclusion that in most instances, the Bible teaches temperance not abstinence. I had to work through that issue also because again I found myself being judgmental when I would see Christians having a glass of wine at a restaurant. However, after I wrote what I did about temperance, I received a polite but firm letter from a dear lady who really took me to task. She was convinced I was selling out a foundation stone of Christian morals. I understand her concern, but she did not give me any evidence from Scripture. It was her personal conviction.

Please don't get me wrong. I think because of the widespread abuse of alcohol in our society today there are some good reasons for practicing abstinence. And in another context I could make a strong argument for abstinence based on those concerns. But this chapter is about judgmentalism, and I'm just giving some first-person examples of how easy it is to become judgmental over issues the Bible does not address or address with the clarity we would like.

The apostle Paul faced this problem head-on in Romans 14. Apparently, there were two specific issues calculated to spawn judgmentalism in the church at Rome. One was vegetarianism versus an "eat whatever you want" mentality. The second issue was a matter of observing certain days as holy days. In Paul's words, "One person esteems one day as better than another, while another esteems all days alike" (Romans 14:5).

Apparently, the people who ate only vegetables were judgmental toward those who ate anything (presumably meat), while those who ate anything despised — probably in the sense of being contemptuous — those who ate only vegetables (see verse 3). Both sides were judgmental toward the other. The vegetarians thought they had the moral high ground and so looked down their religious noses at those who ate anything. The other side thought they had superior knowledge. They *knew* that what they ate made no difference to God if it was received with thanksgiving (see 1 Timothy 4:4). So they were judgmental in a different way.

There are similar attitudes today. Contemporary music advocates may disdain those who prefer traditional music as simply old-fashioned and out of touch with the times. As one young pastor said to me, "With our music we're going to get all

165

the young people out of your church." They can be as judgmental in a reverse sort of way as those who hold out for the traditional hymns. The same is true with the issue of temperance versus abstinence. I have known of instances where those who regard the use of alcohol as a matter of Christian liberty, are contemptuous toward those who practice abstinence.

My point here is that it doesn't matter which side of an issue we are on. It is easy to become judgmental toward anyone whose opinions are different from ours. And then we hide our judgmentalism under the cloak of Christian convictions.

Paul's response to the situation in Rome was, "Stop judging one another regardless of which position you take." And then he added, "Who are you to pass judgment on the servant of another. It is before his own master that he stands or falls. And he will be upheld, for the Lord is able to make Him stand" (Romans 14:4). Basically, Paul was saying, "Stop trying to play God toward your fellow believers in Christ. God is the Judge, not you."

That's what we're doing when we judge others whose preferences and practices are different from ours. We are arrogating to ourselves a role God has reserved for Himself. Perhaps this is what Jesus had in mind in the well-known passage Matthew 7:1-5 when He said, "Why do you see the speck that is in your brother's eye, but do not notice the log that is in your own eye?" Could it be that the log in our own eye is the log of judgmentalism, arrogating to ourselves the role of God?

Here again we see Jesus using hyperbole to make His point. Physically, it is impossible to have a log in one's eye. But just as the ten thousand talents in the parable of the unforgiving servant represents the true extent of our sin against God, so the log in one's own eye may well represent God's verdict on our sin of judgmentalism. If I'm correct, then the seriousness of the sin of judgmentalism is not so much that I judge my brother as that in so doing I assume the role of God.

What I've written to this point does not mean that we

should never pass judgment on the practices and beliefs of others. When someone's lifestyle or conduct is clearly out of line with the Scriptures, then we are right to say that the person is sinning. There are practices that are clearly condemned in Scripture. See, for example, the description of the moral slide into utter depravity that Paul describes in Romans 1:24-32. Or look at his description of the "works of the flesh" (see Galatians 5:19-21), or the characteristics of "the last days" (see 2 Timothy 3:1-5). These practices are clearly sinful. And when we judge them as such, we are simply agreeing with the Word of God. It is the Bible that is judging, not ourselves.

Having said that, though, we can still sin even when we judge in accordance with Scripture. We can sin if we judge from an attitude of self-righteousness or if we judge harshly or with a spirit of censoriousness. We sin if we condemn the obviously flagrant sins of others without at the same time acknowledging that we ourselves are still sinners before God. One of the major objectives of this book is to help us stop doing that.

## DOCTRINAL JUDGMENTALISM

Another area where we can easily slip into the spirit of judgmentalism is that of doctrinal differences. For many evangelicals today this is a nonissue, because for them, doctrine is not important. I remember when I took a stand against open theism, the belief that God does not and cannot know the future. One friend said to me, "Why get so disturbed about this? Why can't we just all love Jesus and get along with one another?"

Many of us, however, know that doctrine is important; and because we believe that is true, we can easily fall into the sin of judgmentalism. For example, the doctrine of Christ's substitutionary atonement for our sins and the complementary doctrine of justification by faith in Christ alone are, to me, crucial doctrines. These are the kind of doctrines where I, so to speak, draw a line in the sand and say, "No compromise. None whatsoever, period!" However, some writers and teachers who consider themselves evangelicals are denying Christ's substitutionary atonement. To them, Christ did not die in our place to pay for our sins. Instead, He went to the cross solely as an example for us to follow when we suffer. Others downplay the death of Christ on the cross, saying we should not focus on the cross of Christ but rather on His life, which we should follow as an example. Whenever the subject of my teaching or speaking warrants it, I take issue with these folks. And I think I am right in doing so. But I confess I have at times slipped into the sin of judgmentalism. I disagree so strongly with what they are teaching that I have sometimes demonized them. I don't think I'm alone in this sin. I've observed it happening among others within our evangelical community. Because we do believe so strongly in the importance of sound doctrine, we can easily become hypercritical of those with whom we disagree. We should express our disagreements, but we should do so in a way that does not degenerate into character assassination.

## A CRITICAL SPIRIT

Most of us can slip into the sin of judgmentalism from time to time. But there are those among us who practice it continually. These people have what I call *a critical spirit*. They look for and find fault with everyone and everything. Regardless of the topic of conversation — whether it's a person, a church, an event, or anything — they end up speaking in a disparaging manner. I'm not writing about theoretical people. I've been with some of them, and they are not pleasant to be around.

In earlier sessions, I have mentioned that some of our acceptable sins, such as selfishness, impatience, and anger, are often expressed more freely at home among our family members than in public, especially the Christian public. This can also be true in this area of judgmentalism. Sometimes a spouse, either the husband or wife, can be a continual faultfinder toward the other or toward one or more of the children. The object of such continual criticism begins to think he or she can't do anything right.

A friend of mine tells of being raised in an upper-middle-class Christian home where the father was hypercritical, especially of the middle child, a daughter. She gradually developed into a person who "could not do anything right" — at least one would think as much to hear her dad berate her. But the more he criticized her posture, the more she slumped. The more he pointed out her lack of eye contact, the more her eyes became fixed and down-gazed. If his repeatedly putting her down "for her own good" had one result, it was a type of self-fulfilling prophecy. She felt her father's pattern of criticism as rejection, and she came to see herself as a reject. As an adult, her number one priority became to seek out those who would provide her with acceptance, and her "friends" soon learned how to take advantage of her need to be accepted. On his deathbed, the father realized his sinfulness and tearfully repented of his critical spirit toward his daughter. But it was too late. By then she had secretly become promiscuous and a crack cocaine addict.

This is an extreme example of the destructive nature of speaking from a critical and judgmental spirit. But there is plenty of evidence all around us of this sin's sinfulness. It is often said that it takes seven compliments to undo the effects of one criticism. So let's examine ourselves; or better yet, let's subject ourselves to the examination of others. Do we have a critical spirit? Do we continually find fault with others, especially members of our own family or members of our own church?

Finally, I suspect that some of my dearest friends may disagree with some things I've said in this chapter. Some do not see the manner of dress in church or the type of music we sing as matters of preference. For them, it is a conviction. I respect their thinking and wouldn't want to change their convictions at all.

I'd like to be like Paul, who took a similar position regarding the divisive issues in Rome. He did not try to change anyone's convictions regarding what they ate or the special days they observed. Instead, he said, "Each one should be fully convinced in his own mind" (Romans 14:5). Such a statement makes many of us uncomfortable. We don't like ambiguity in issues of Christian practice. It's difficult for us to accept that one person's opinion can be different from ours and both of us be accepted by God. But that is what Paul says in Romans 14. And if we will take Paul seriously and hold our convictions with humility, it will help us avoid the sin of judgmentalism.

---

## Chapter Seventeen: Sins of the Tongue

In the months that I have been working on this book, I have often been asked in social settings, "What are you working on now?" When I mention the "respectable" or "acceptable" sins we tolerate, invariably someone will roll his or her eyes and say, "Oh, you mean like gossip." Apparently, this is the first of the Christian sins that comes to mind, so it must be quite prevalent among us and is something we continue to tolerate in our lives.

As widespread as the practice of gossip is, however, it is by no means the only sin of the tongue. In this category, we must also include lying, slander, critical speech (even when true), harsh words, insults, sarcasm, and ridicule. In fact, we would have to say that any speech that tends to tear down another person — either someone we are talking about or someone we are talking to — is sinful speech.

The Bible is replete with warnings against sins of the tongue. The book of Proverbs alone contains about sixty such warnings. Jesus warned that we will give account for every careless word we speak (see Matthew 12:36). And then there is that well-known passage in James 3 where he speaks of the sinful effects of the tongue. He likens those effects to a small fire that sets the forest ablaze and a member that stains the whole body.

The passage of Scripture that has helped me most to deal with the sins of the tongue, however, is Ephesians 4:29: "Let no corrupting talk come out of your mouths, but only such as is good for building up, as fits the occasion, that it may give grace to those who hear."

This verse is an application of Paul's "put off / put on" principle that he sets forth in Ephesians 4:22-24. The principle is that we are to put off the sinful traits of the old self and, at the same time, give diligence to putting on the gracious traits of the new self created in Christ.

As we look at Ephesians 4:29, we see that we are not to let any corrupting talk come out of our mouths. Corrupting talk is not limited to profanity or obscene speech. It includes all the various types of negative speech I mentioned previously. Note Paul's absolute prohibition. *No* corrupting talk. None whatsoever. This means *no* gossip, *no* sarcasm, *no* critical speech, *no* harsh words. All of these sinful words that tend to tear down another person must be put out of our speech. Think about what the church of Jesus Christ would look like if we all sought to apply Paul's words.

As we think of sins of the tongue, let's begin with the one most people think of first: gossip. Gossip is the spreading of unfavorable information about someone else, even if that information is true. However, gossip is often based on rumor, which makes the sin even worse. Indulging in gossip seems to feed our sinful ego, especially when the information we're passing along is negative. It makes us feel self-righteous by comparison. And then there are those times when we disguise our gossip as, "I want to share this with you for your prayers." If we know something negative about someone, we should pray about it. But we should not spread around the bad news.

Ephesians 4:29 not only tells us what kinds of speech to

put off, it also tells us what to put on. It is only such speech that builds up and gives grace to those who hear it. Therefore, when we are tempted to gossip, we should ask ourselves, *Will what I'm about to say tend to tear down or build up the person I'm about to talk about?*

Closely related to the sin of gossip is the sin of slander. Slander is making a false statement or misrepresentation about another person that defames or damages the person's reputation. Political campaigns, for example, are notorious for slandering opponents by falsely ascribing to the opponent a position based on statements taken out of context or based on some isolated act that occurred some years ago. It is such statements that are definitely aimed at creating a false, slanderous impression.

But do Christians slander? Yes, we do. We slander when we ascribe wrong motives to people, even though we can't see their hearts or know their particular circumstances. We slander when we say another believer is "not committed" when he or she does not practice the same spiritual disciplines we do or engage in the same Christian activities we engage in. We slander when we misrepresent another person's position on a subject without first determining what that person's position is. We slander when we blow out of proportion another person's sin and make that person appear to be more sinful than he or she really is.

The motive behind slander is often to gain an advantage in some way over another person. In the business world, it is called "backstabbing" or "climbing the corporate ladder over other people's backs." But sometimes we Christians can do this kind of thing. In a Christian organization or a church, we can seek to gain an advantage over someone else by slandering that person.

Slander is actually lying. But there are, of course, other forms of lying. We usually think of it as making a false statement, and probably most of us tend to guard against such speech. However, we are apt to lie by exaggeration, by a failure to tell the whole truth, or by indulging in what we call a "little white lie" — a lie that we think is of no consequence. Whatever

Notes and Observations

form it takes, a lie expresses an intent to deceive. A good test we might use of our speech is the question, "Is it true?"

Critical speech is negative comments about someone that may be actually true but doesn't need to be said. For example, "He spends too much time watching television" or "She's not a good student." The questions we should ask ourselves about these kinds of comments are *Is it kind?* and *Is it needful?* By the latter, I mean does it really need to be said?

We not only sin in our speech *about* one another but we also sin when talking *to* one another. This sinful speech includes harsh words, sarcasm, insults, and ridicule. The common denominator of all these forms of negative speech is that they tend to put down, humiliate, or hurt the other person. This type of speech most often comes from an attitude of impatience or anger. Jesus said, "Out of the abundance of the heart the mouth speaks" (Matthew 12:34). This means that although we speak of sins of the tongue, our real problem is our heart. Behind all of our gossip, slander, critical speech, insults, and sarcasm is our sinful heart. The tongue is only the instrument that reveals what's in our hearts.

For some years I have sought to apply Ephesians 4:29 to my speech. I'm sure I fail many times, but at least that's the benchmark, or target, I aim for. One night I started to say something negative to my wife about a former colleague. But then I thought of Ephesians 4:29, and, as we say, "I bit my tongue." I felt quite good about my self-control until the next morning. During my time with God, I thought about the previous night's incident. Then the thought came to me, "But you thought it, didn't you?" I was brought up short. I realized I needed to guard not only my mouth, but more important, I needed to guard my heart.

David prayed, "Let the words of my mouth and the meditation of my heart be acceptable in your sight, O LORD, my rock and my redeemer" (Psalm 19:14). David was concerned not only with his words but also with the thoughts of his heart. I have learned to pray this also. I still use Ephesians 4:29 as a guideline, but now I try to apply it to my thoughts as well as my speech. I'd like to have no corrupting thoughts come out of my heart but only thoughts, if uttered, that would build up those who hear them.

If you and I truly want to put on the new self created after the likeness of God in true righteousness and holiness, we must make Ephesians 4:29 one of our guiding principles.

So take a few moments to reflect on this chapter and your own speech patterns. Do you gossip or criticize others or tend to show impatience or anger through unkind words that tend to humiliate or hurt the person who is the object of your impatience or anger? Better yet, ask your friends or, if married, your spouse or older children. Remember, we're talking about real sin. The kind of speech we've discussed in this chapter may seem acceptable to us, but it is not acceptable to God. It truly is sin.

# Judgmentalism and Sins of the Tongue

## (Chapters 16 and 17)

## STUDY QUESTIONS

KEY VERSES: "There is only one lawgiver and judge, he who is able to save and to destroy. But who are you to judge your neighbor? . . . Let no corrupting talk come out of your mouths, but only such as is good for building up, as fits the occasion, that it may give grace to those who hear." (James 4:12; Ephesians 4:29)

## GET FOCUSED

If you were to gather one hundred church people from a variety of ages and lifestyles and ask which type of church music is best and what the "dress code" of a church should be, disagreement would erupt. Why? Because we often equate our opinions with truth and quickly judge people who disagree with us. This leads to the "respectable" sin of judgmentalism. "How easy it is," Jerry Bridges writes, "to become judgmental over issues the Bible does not address or address with the clarity we would like."

As we'll realize during this session, personal preferences are quite different from Bible-based convictions and God's clear commands. Clearly there are moments where it is best to agree to disagree. For example, the Bible doesn't tell us what kind of music to listen to. And when we need to humbly defend key biblical doctrines and challenge believers whose lifestyle or conduct is clearly out of line with the Bible, we need to avoid demonizing or becoming hypercritical of those with whom we disagree.

"Respectable" sins of the tongue — gossip, negative words, slander, and so on — are also common within the church and our culture. Even though they are often tolerated and even encouraged, these sins are incredibly damaging. Fortunately God gives His followers His power so we can "put on our new selves" — created after His likeness in true righteousness and holiness.

THINK IT THROUGH
FOR PERSONAL STUDY

### I. Judgmentalism

1. "Judgmentalism begins," writes the author, when "we equate our opinions with truth." What's the difference between a preference for something (a certain kind of food, for example) and a Bible-based conviction? What can happen when we elevate personal convictions concerning an issue to the level of biblical truth — even when the Bible is not clear on that particular issue?

2. "It is easy," the author writes, "to become judgmental toward anyone whose opinions are different from ours." Think of a time when you've seen this happen. What consequences occurred?

3. Paul faced judgmentalism head-on (see Romans 14). One group in the church at Rome ate only vegetables and thought they had the moral high ground (see 14:3); another group ate "anything" (presumably meat) and thought they had superior knowledge because what they ate made no difference to God if it was received with thanksgiving (1 Timothy 4:4). And each group judged the other. In addition, some believers observed certain days as holy days, and other believers did not.

a. Read Romans 14:4-5. How would you describe Paul's response?

b. What position did Paul take concerning the personal convictions of what people ate or special days they observed?

4. "Because we do believe so strongly in the importance of sound doctrine," Jerry writes, "we can easily become hypercritical of those with whom we disagree." What do you think is the proper balance between (a) standing up for key biblical doctrine, and (b) expressing disagreement with advocates of unsound doctrine in ways that do not degenerate into character assassination?

## II. *Sins of the Tongue*

1. How do we know that God takes "respectable" sins of the tongue seriously? (See Matthew 12:36-37.)

2. "Any speech," the author writes, "that tends to tear down another person — either someone we are talking about or someone we are talking to — is sinful speech." Do you agree or disagree? Why?

3. Read Ephesians 4:29. Describe, in your own words, what God (through Paul) tells us to do. How does this verse relate to the "put off/put on" principle Paul mentioned earlier in verses 22-24?

4. Which word picture(s) did James use (see James 3:1-12) to illustrate the tongue's power and sinful effects? What did he want us to realize?

## TALK IT OVER
## FOR GROUP DISCUSSION

1. Biblically, when should we pass judgment on the practices and beliefs of other believers? What criteria must we use? (Read Romans 1:24-32; Galatians 5:19-21; 2 Timothy 3:1-5.) How is the perspective of Bible-based confrontation different from much of our society's emphasis on "tolerance"?

2. What dangers do we face when we judge others whose preferences and practices are different from ours? When do we need to pass Bible-based judgment on the practices and beliefs of a believer whose lifestyle or conduct is clearly not in line with the Scriptures?

3. How have Christians' judgmentalism and sinful speech affected their churches? Their witness in the local community?

4. Jerry writes: "Note Paul's absolute prohibition [in Ephesians 4:29]. *No* corrupting talk. None whatsoever. This means *no* gossip, *no* sarcasm, *no* critical speech, *no* harsh words. . . . Think about what the church of Jesus Christ would look like if we all sought to apply Paul's words." If indeed we could live and worship together in this way, what *would* the body of Christ be like? What are we each willing to do in order to help make that happen?

5. How can we disagree strongly with people who undermine key biblical doctrine, such as Jesus' substitutionary atonement for our sins, while not committing judgmentalism?

6. What is the real problem and source of our sinful speech? (See Matthew 12:33; Luke 6:45.)

## GROUP PRAYER

As a group, pray together this prayer of David (Psalm 19:14): "Let the words of my mouth and the meditation of my heart be acceptable in your sight, O LORD, my rock and my redeemer."

❧ ❧

FOR NEXT TIME: Read *Respectable Sins*, chapters 18 and 19, and then respond to the "Think It Through" personal-study questions for session 8.

## TAKE IT TO HEART

*A PERSONAL-GROWTH JOURNAL*

### *Personal Reflection*

How do you feel when you are with someone who continually practices judgmentalism — having a critical spirit and finding fault with everyone and everything? Why do you think a critical spirit is so damaging?

Which sins of the tongue tempt you the most?

"The tongue," writes the author, "is only the instrument that reveals what's in our hearts." Based on your speech, what is in your heart? What might the Holy Spirit be prompting you to do about it?

### *Personal Action Point*

For the next two days, ask yourself, Will what I'm about to say tend to tear down or build up the person to whom I speak (or about whom I speak)?

### *Personal Prayer*

Confess any sins of judgmentalism or sins of the tongue. Talk honestly with God about how you'd like to improve, and invite Him to help you.

---

## PROGRESS REPORT

How aware are you becoming of your "respectable" sins, including judgmentalism and sins of the tongue?

What are you willing to do in order to remain focused on these types of sins now that this study is drawing to a close? What benefits will you receive if you do this — spiritually, relationally, vocationally?

Share one "take-away" that has affected you the most during the previous seven sessions, and why it is so significant.

Which key Scripture or important principle from this study might you share with other people?

# Lack of Self-Control, Envy, and Jealousy

BEFORE GATHERING: Read the following portion of *Respectable Sins*. In the margins, record observations, illustrations, or questions that come to mind as you read. Then answer the "Think It Through" study questions that follow the reading.

---

## Chapter Eighteen: Lack of Self-Control

*Notes and Observations*

"A man without self-control is like a city broken into and left without walls" (Proverbs 25:28). In biblical times, a city's walls were its chief means of defense. If the walls were breached, an invading army could pour into the city and conquer it. We recall from the account of the fall of Jericho that God caused its walls to collapse so that the army of Israel could easily move in and take the city (see Joshua 6:1-5,20).

In the same way that a city without walls was vulnerable to an invading army, so a person without self-control is vulnerable to all kinds of temptations. Unfortunately, Solomon, who wrote those words in Proverbs 25:28, is a sad but striking demonstration of his own words. The Scriptures record that Solomon had seven hundred wives and three hundred concubines, all from nations concerning which the Lord had said to the people of Israel that they should not take wives (see 1 Kings 11:1-3). But Solomon gave free reign to his passions and totally disregarded God's prohibition. As the wealthiest potentate of that era, Solomon had access to all he might desire. But instead of exercising self-control, he disregarded his own words of wisdom and let his passions run out of control. Solomon paid a heavy price for his lack of self-control. His wives turned his heart away from God. Because of that, God divided Solomon's

181

kingdom in the days of his son Rehoboam, and the Davidic dynasty was crippled from that time forward.

The Scriptures, both in Proverbs and the letters of the New Testament, have a lot to say about self-control. Paul lists it as one expression of the fruit of the Spirit (see Galatians 5:22-23), and he includes a lack of self-control in the list of vices characteristic of the last days (see 2 Timothy 3:3). His instructions to Titus regarding his ministry in Crete included several exhortations to teach self-control (see Titus 2:2,5,6), and a reminder that the same grace that brings salvation also trains us to live self-controlled lives (see Titus 2:11-12). Then Peter urges us to be sober-minded, or self-controlled, several times in his two letters (see 1 Peter 1:13; 4:7; 5:8; 2 Peter 1:5).

Despite the scriptural teaching on self-control, I suspect this is one virtue that receives little *conscious* attention from most Christians. We have boundaries from our Christian culture that tend to restrain us from obvious sins, but within those boundaries we pretty much live as we please. We seldom say "no" to our desires and emotions. A lack of self-control may well be one of our more "respectable" sins. And because we tolerate this, we become more vulnerable to other "respectable" sins. A lack of control of our tongue, for example, opens the door to all manner of defiling speech such as sarcasm, gossip, slander, and ridicule.

What is self-control? It is a governance or prudent control of one's desires, cravings, impulses, emotions, and passions. It is saying no when we should say no. It is moderation in legitimate desires and activities, and absolute restraint in areas that are clearly sinful. It would, for example, involve moderation in watching television and absolute restraint in viewing Internet pornography.

Biblical self-control is not a product of one's own natural willpower. We know there are plenty of unbelievers who exercise self-control in specific areas of life for the purpose of achieving some goal. But in other areas, they may live with little or no self-control. An athlete may be strict in his diet while totally lacking in control of his temper.

Biblical self-control, however, covers every area of life and requires an unceasing conflict with the passions of the flesh that wage war against our souls (see 1 Peter 2:11). This self-control is dependent on the influence and enablement of the Holy Spirit. It requires continual exposure of our mind to the words of God and continual prayer for the Holy Spirit to give us both the desire and power to exercise self-control. We might say that self-control is not control *by* oneself through one's own willpower but rather control *of* oneself through the power of the Holy Spirit.

Though self-control needs to be exercised in all areas of life, in this chapter we will look at three areas where Christians often fail to exercise it. The first is the area of *eating and drinking*. Let me say right away that I am not singling out those who have a so-called "weight problem." That may or may not be due to a lack of self-control. One of the most self-controlled men I have ever known struggled with his weight all his adult life. On the other hand, some who can eat what they please without gaining weight may, because of that fact, fail to exercise self-control in their eating and drinking.

What I am addressing is the tendency to continually give in to our desires for certain foods or drinks. I think of an acquaintance, a committed Christian, who used to consume twelve cans of soda every day. I think of my own craving for ice cream years ago when I would have a dish of it at dinner and another at bedtime. In that situation, God convicted me of my lack of self-control by causing me to see that a seemingly benign practice greatly weakened my self-control in other more critical areas. I learned that we cannot pick and choose the areas of life in which we will exercise self-control.

One of the ways we can exercise self-control is by removing or getting away from whatever tempts us to indulge our desires. In the case of the ice cream, I asked my wife to no longer keep it regularly in the freezer. Instead, we now buy it for specific occasions. Even though I made that decision more than thirty years ago, I still have to exercise self-control. Recently I was on my way to mail a package at a contract post office that is located in an ice cream shop. As I drove, I began to think about having a dish of ice cream. As I wrestled with that strong desire, I concluded that it was a time when I needed to say "no" to myself just for the purpose of keeping that desire under control.

I'm not trying to lay a guilt trip on those who enjoy ice cream or soda pop, or even those who go to Starbucks every day for their favorite coffee drink. What I am addressing is our lack of self-control — a tendency to indulge our desires so that they control us, instead of our controlling those desires.

A second area where Christians often show a lack of self-control is with one's *temper*. Some believers are known to be hot-tempered or to have a short fuse. A hot temper is a quick but intense burst of anger often followed soon afterward by a calm disposition. A person with a short fuse is a person who tends to become easily angry or irritable and who exercises little or no control over his emotions. Quite often a person who is hot-tempered also has a short fuse. Our expression for such a person is "He easily flies off the handle."

We have already addressed the issue of anger in session 6, but here the focus is on one's lack of self-control over his anger. Anger, in most instances, is sin, but with the short-tempered person, there is the added sin of a lack of self-control.

Outbursts of temper are usually directed against anyone who displeases us. It may be another driver who cuts us off on the freeway or an umpire who makes a bad call at a church softball game. Unfortunately, it is often directed toward one's own family members.

There are a number of warnings against a quick temper in Proverbs. For example, "A man of quick temper acts foolishly" (Proverbs 14:17) and "Whoever is slow to anger is better than the mighty, and he who rules his spirit than he who takes a city"

(Proverbs 16:32). In the New Testament, James admonishes us to be "slow to anger" (1:19). Remember, we are to store up God's Word in our hearts that we might not sin against Him (see Psalm 119:11). We can store up these verses from Proverbs and James to help us exercise self-control over our tempers.

A third area where many Christians lack self-control is in the area of *personal finances*. Recently I heard a national radio speaker say that the average American household has a credit card debt of $7,000. Undoubtedly there are times when an individual or family may get into that kind of debt because of an emergency situation. But the fact that $7,000 is the *average* debt indicates that Americans are spending beyond their means. As a nation, we are not exercising financial self-control; rather, we are indulging our desires for what we want: new clothes, the latest electronic or digital devices, expensive vacations, and a host of other goods and services that appeal to our desires.

That this is a problem among Christians is attested by the fact that several Christian ministries are dedicated to the purpose of helping Christians get control of their finances. They are simply helping people learn to exercise self-control.

However, it is not just those in debt who fail to exercise self-control over their spending. Many affluent people, including some Christians, indulge themselves in whatever their hearts desire. They are like the writer of Ecclesiastes (presumably Solomon), who said, "Whatever my eyes desired I did not keep from them" (2:10). Indulging in whatever my heart desires, even if I can easily afford it, is not the way to gain that self-control, which is a fruit of the Spirit (more on this in session 9, chapter 20).

There are other areas in which we may need to learn self-control. I think of the person who spends an inordinate amount of time at his computer, even if not viewing pornography. Other areas would include watching television, impulse buying, engaging in hobbies, and playing or watching various sports. For men, a big need for self-control is over our eyes and thought lives in this age of increasingly immodest dress.

Notes and Observations

No doubt there are other areas that can easily lend themselves to a lack of self-control, so I encourage you to reflect on your own life. Are there desires, cravings, or emotions that may be out of control to some degree? Remember, this book is about "respectable" or "acceptable" sins, the sins we tolerate in our lives. And because the virtue of self-control receives so little emphasis among Christians, we may find that we, at least in certain areas of life, do lack self-control. As you seek to grow in the area of self-control, remember it is a fruit of the Spirit (see Galatians 5:22-23). It is only by God's enabling power that we can make any progress.

---

## Chapter Nineteen:
### Envy, Jealousy, and Related Sins

I recently learned that a friend who has written about as many books as I have receives frequent requests for speaking engagements from all over the world. When I heard that, I thought to myself, *I have written as many books as she has. Why don't I receive those kinds of invitations?* I was tempted, though only briefly, to be envious of her.

*Envy* is the painful and oftentimes resentful awareness of an advantage enjoyed by someone else. Sometimes we want that same advantage, leading to the further sin of covetousness. And sometimes we just resent the other person having something we don't have. But we don't just envy people in general. Usually, there are two conditions that tempt us to envy. First, we tend to envy those with whom we most closely identify. Second, we tend to envy in them the areas we value most.

My friend meets both of these criteria. We both labor in the same arena — teaching and writing, which is an area of high value to me. We both have enjoyed some measure of blessing on our work, but neither of us has become what I would call a "high profile" writer or teacher. So I identify with her as a fellow writer and teacher of more or less equal standing in an area that I highly value.

What, then, prompted the temptation to envy? It was that she was enjoying an advantage I didn't have. She is getting all these international speaking invitations, while I receive almost none. The irony is that I don't enjoy overseas travel. I don't like the long flights or going through immigration or dealing with foreign currency or being among people whose language I don't understand. So why was I tempted to envy my friend? It was because she was getting more recognition than I was. Do you see how subtle the temptation to envy can be?

I am never tempted to envy musicians or artists or highly successful business and professional people. I may admire some of them, but I don't envy them. Their talents and expertise are completely different from mine, so I don't tend to compare myself with them. And even within the areas of teaching and writing, there are so many who are obviously much more gifted than I am that envy of them is not an issue for me. They work in the area of high value for me, but they are so far beyond me that I cannot identify with them.

Consider a young baseball player in the minor leagues hoping to someday make it to the majors. He doesn't envy the major league stars. They are out of his league. But he might envy a fellow team member who is moving up faster than he is, especially if he believes the other player is receiving favor from the team manager. An insurance salesman is not likely to envy a professional athlete who earns a multimillion-dollar salary. But he may well envy another salesman who sells more insurance than he does. A pastor of a small- or medium-size church is not likely to envy the mega-church pastor. But he may be tempted to envy the pastor down the street whose church is growing more than his. The reason we are tempted to envy in these situations is that there are enough things alike that the differences tend to strike us in the face.

Parents may envy other parents whose children are better students or athletes or, if adults, have better jobs. We may envy friends who have a nicer home or drive a more expensive car. The possibilities for envy are endless. Whenever we compare ourselves with anyone whose circumstances seem better than ours, we face the temptation to envy him or her. We may not even want the better circumstances of our neighbor or friend; we just resent their having them. But when we are tempted to envy, we should realize that envy, though it may be a subtle and seemingly minor sin to us, is listed among the vile sins that Paul catalogues in Romans 1:29 and Galatians 5:21.

## JEALOUSY

Closely akin to envy is the sin of jealousy. In fact, we often equate these two words and treat them as synonyms. But there is a subtle distinction between them that will again help us see the sinfulness of our hearts. *Jealousy* is usually defined as intolerance of rivalry. There are legitimate occasions for jealousy, such as when someone is trying to win your spouse away from you. God even declares Himself to be a jealous God who will not tolerate the worship of anyone or anything other than Himself (see Exodus 20:5). Sinful jealousy occurs, however, when we are afraid someone is going to become equal to or even superior to us.

There are several illustrations of jealousy in the Bible to help us see what it looks like. In the early days of the church when the Jewish authorities still had the upper hand, Luke tells us that the high priests and the Sadducees were filled with jealousy toward the apostles because more and more Jews were turning to Christ (see Acts 5:17-18). Later, during Paul's ministry, Luke records that the Jews of Antioch of Pisidia were jealous of Paul and Barnabas because great crowds were gathering around them to hear Paul preach (see Acts 13:44-45). The classic illustration in the Bible of sinful jealousy is that of King Saul's jealousy of David. After David slew Goliath, the women of Israel sang, "Saul

Notes and Observations

has struck down his thousands, and David his ten thousands"
(1 Samuel 18:7). Saul became angry because they ascribed more
honor to David than him. From that time onward, he regarded
David as a rival and was jealous of him.

We, too, can be jealous if we have been blessed of God
in some area of life or ministry and then someone comes
along whose performance or results are superior to ours. Let's
assume that Ben, a car salesman, has been quite successful and
has been the top salesperson at his dealership for three years.
But then a new salesperson comes along who rapidly overtakes
Ben. He begins to receive the recognition and awards that
formerly went to Ben. Very likely, Ben will now be tempted to
become jealous.

Ben's situation happens all the time. There always seems to
be a younger person coming along who is smarter or more talented or more gifted than we are. When that happens, many of
us experience jealousy. We don't want someone else to experience the success or blessing of God that we have experienced.

How, then, can we deal with the temptation to envy or
to become jealous? First of all, we can, as in so many other
areas of subtle sins, turn to the sovereignty of God. We must
recognize that it is God who sovereignly gives us our talents,
abilities, and spiritual gifts. If we are to successfully combat
the temptations to envy and jealousy, we must mentally bring
God into the picture. We must remind ourselves that He
determines not only what abilities we have but also the degree
of those abilities and the blessing He will bestow on their use.
It's obvious as we look around that some are better car salesmen than others. Some are more gifted pastors. Some men are
more talented in working with their hands in the building and
mechanical trades. Not only are there differing talents and
gifts but also there is a widespread diversity in God's blessing on those gifts. All this is from God, who makes poor and
makes rich, who brings low and exalts (see 1 Samuel 2:7). It is
God who puts down one and exalts another (see Psalm 75:7).

We must recognize that to be envious or jealous of someone is either eliminating God from the picture or else accusing Him of being unfair.

A second weapon against the temptation to envy or become jealous is to remember that all of us who are believers are "one body in Christ and individually members one of another," or as the NIV translates it, "Each member belongs to all the others" (Romans 12:5). Therefore, Paul says to us, "Outdo one another in showing honor" (verse 10). Instead of being envious of those who have some advantage over us or being jealous of those who may be overtaking us in some way, we should honor and applaud them, for we are all members of the same body in Christ.

Third, we should realize that if we spend emotional energy on envy or jealousy, we lose sight of what God might do uniquely in our lives. To use athletic metaphors, there is no such thing as being second- or third-stringer on the team or sitting on the bench while others play the game. No, God has a place and an assignment for each of us that He wants us to fill. Admittedly, some assignments garner more human recognition than others, but all are important in the plan of God.

## COMPETITIVENESS

Closely allied with envy and jealousy is the spirit of competitiveness—the urge to always win or be the top person in whatever our field of endeavor is. The competitive urge begins at an early age. Young children can become quite upset or angry when they don't win a simple children's game. But it isn't just children who have a problem. I've seen grown men who were in other respects exemplary Christians lose their temper when they lost or their son's team lost a ball game. Competitiveness is basically an expression of selfishness. It's the urge to win at someone else's expense. It is certainly not loving our neighbor as ourselves.

I realize I'm questioning a "sacred cow" in our culture, because we have elevated competitiveness to a virtue. We teach children directly and by example that it is good to be competitive, that this is the way one gets ahead in the world.

I question, however, whether a competitive spirit is a Christian virtue. I believe the scriptural emphasis is on the virtue of doing one's best (see, for example, 2 Timothy 2:15). In our work, we are to work heartily (see Colossians 3:23), which is another way of saying, "Do your best." But, of course, "our best" is not the same for everyone. Some have been blessed with greater skills or intelligence or spiritual giftedness. And of course always seeking to do our best should be motivated by a desire to glorify God, not win recognition for ourselves. The recognition may come, but it should not be our motivation.

Therefore, Ben the car salesman should concentrate on doing his best to sell cars in a God-honoring way. If his best makes him the top salesman in the dealership, he should not be proud but grateful to God for giving him the ability. If his best puts him third or fourth or whatever in the ranking of salesmen, he can take solace in the fact that he did his best.

Someone may argue that Paul tacitly endorsed competitiveness in 1 Corinthians 9:24: "Do you not know that in a race all the runners compete, but only one receives the prize? So run that you may obtain it." But the analogy breaks down at the point of the prize. In a race, only one runner wins and receives the prize. But in the Christian life, we may all receive the prize. Paul is not urging us to compete with one another. Rather, he is saying, "Run the Christian race with the same intensity that the runners run who are competing for the one prize."

Let me clarify that I'm not writing against friendly competition but against the competitive spirit that always has to win or be the best. Actually, I believe that healthy competition is good, especially for children and high schoolers, as it can provide an arena in which they can seek to do their best. And this kind of competition is not limited to sports. There is competition at science fairs or among bands or at spelling bees. But in whatever competition, the question the child or teenager and their parents should ask is not "Did we win?" but "Did we do our best?"

You can see now that there is a close relationship between envy, jealousy, and competitiveness. We tend to envy a peer who is ahead of us in an area we value highly. We become jealous of a person who is overtaking us. And both of these foster a competitive spirit that says, "I must always win or be number one." All of these attitudes are the result of ungodly selfishness, of thinking only of ourselves.

## CONTROLLING

Envy, jealousy, and competitiveness all may be grouped under one word: *rivalry*. Instead of viewing each other as fellow members of the body of Christ, we can easily slip into the attitude of viewing them as rivals we are competing against. There is one more subtle sin that we may include in this group. That is the sin of seeking to control others to our advantage or to get what we want.

I once asked a pastor about the source of friction between a couple in his church. Without hesitation, he replied, "She wants to control everything. She always wants to get her way." In using this illustration, I'm not singling out women as the always-guilty ones. Men and women both are apt to be controllers. In most ongoing interpersonal relationships, there is one who usually has the stronger or more dominant personality. And if that person is not watchful, he or she can control the relationship. This is true not only in a marriage but in any situation where two or more people are working or playing closely together. You see it in children as they play games. Often one wants to make all the decisions and will get angry if he doesn't get his way.

I have seen this controller mindset at work in a local church where one strong-willed musician continually "fought" the decisions of the church music director. This type of situation is not unique. A friend recently told me of a similar situation at his church. I have another friend, a former pastor and now a missionary, who resigned a pastorate after only six months because one strong-willed family always wanted things done their way. I have even observed it in student ministries at university campuses.

The controller will seek to get his or her way using various methods. One way is to completely dominate a relationship by sheer force of willpower so that the other person (or persons) always gives in and lets him get his way. Another is to get angry when his decisions are questioned or his desires are not readily granted. Often when the controller-type person doesn't easily get his way, he will resort to manipulation to achieve that end. This may be done in a way designed to make the other person feel guilty or incompetent. The controlling husband may say something such as "Why is dinner never on time?" when the actual fact is that dinner usually is on time. The manipulative wife might say, "You are just like my father" (because her father wouldn't always let her get her way). In the instance of the musician who wanted to control the church music, the person resorted to character assassination against the music director.

Obviously, the controller wants to get his own way. Instead of submitting to each other (see Ephesians 5:21), there is the urge to control one another. This obviously springs from selfishness. The difficulty in addressing this sin is that the controller is the last one to recognize this tendency in his life.

Since we all still have the flesh waging its guerilla warfare in us, we still have blind spots of sin — especially subtle sin — in our lives. We need the convicting power of the Holy Spirit, and we need the help of others to see those blind spots. So I urge you to ask God to help you see tendencies toward envy or jealousy or competitiveness or controlling others. Ask those closest to you to give you honest feedback. If you are a controller-type person, you may find they are reluctant to do that because of your past behavior. So you must demonstrate a true humility in asking them. Then, instead of becoming defensive — or using

Notes and Observations

it against them — when they are honest with you, wisely accept what they say and take it to God to help you.

I once confronted a controller-type person in our ministry about this tendency in his life (actually, I think I was the third person to do so). Instead of hearing me, he got visibly upset and severed our relationship. He carefully avoided me from that time onward. I have not seen him in some years. But the last I heard of him, he still had the problem. He refused to face his sin.

Don't be like that. Don't go through life harboring envy or jealousy or always having to win or get your way. Remember, "God opposes the proud but gives grace to the humble" (1 Peter 5:5). Don't place yourself in the position of being opposed by God.

# Lack of Self-Control, Envy, and Jealousy

## (Chapters 18 and 19)

## STUDY QUESTIONS

KEY VERSES: "A man without self-control is like a city broken into and left without walls.... The works of the flesh are evident:... jealousy, fits of anger, rivalries, dissensions, divisions, envy." (Proverbs 25:28; Galatians 5:19-21)

## GET FOCUSED

*Self-control* is unpopular in many circles. Our culture offers many temptations and encourages us to fulfill our desires. *Go ahead, experience it. Buy it. Try it. It's your right. You've earned it.*

Through words and personal examples, the Bible says much about self-control. Solomon backslid horribly because he lacked self-control. Other biblical characters lost their tempers, ate to excess during Communion-related meals, and became materialistic. As believers, we experience passions of the flesh that wage war against our souls (see 1 Peter 2:11).

Most of us recognize boundaries that tend to restrain us from obvious sins, but otherwise we pretty much live as we please. Knowing it is easy for us to say yes instead of no, and indulge sinful desires, God emphasizes self-control repeatedly. It is even listed in the fruit of the Spirit (see Galatians 5:22-23). You see, this self-control is not control by our own willpower, but rather control of ourselves through the Holy Spirit's power.

Since humankind's earliest days, envy, jealousy, and related sins — such as sinful competitiveness and trying to control people — have caused great problems. For example, jealous Cain killed Abel (see Genesis 4:1-8). It's easy to respond with envy and jealousy when people enjoy advantages and blessings we don't have, to compare ourselves to others whose circumstances, talents, and giftedness seem better than ours. And to ignore how vile envy and jealousy really are (see Romans 1:29; Galatians 5:20-21).

## THINK IT THROUGH
## FOR PERSONAL STUDY

### *I. Lack of Self-Control*

1. A person lacking self-control is vulnerable to all kinds of temptations. Solomon, who wrote a key verse found at the beginning of this session, illustrates this. What happened to him and the Israelite nation, as recorded in 1 Kings 11:1-6,29-33?

2. What do these verses reveal to you about self-control?

Galatians 5:22-23:

2 Timothy 3:1-3:

Titus 2:2,5-6:

Ecclesiastes 2:10:

3. Because biblical self-control is not a product of our natural willpower, what trains us to live self-controlled lives? (See Titus 2:11-12.) What does this insight mean to you personally?

4. In order for us to exercise self-control, what must we battle unceasingly? (See 1 Peter 2:11.)

5. "Self-control is dependent," Jerry writes, "on the influence and enablement of the Holy Spirit. It requires continual exposure of our mind to the words of God and continual prayer for the Holy Spirit to give us both the desire and power to exercise self-control."

   a. In our individualistic, goal-oriented culture, why is this truth important to remember?

   b. In light of our busy lives, what specific steps can we take to ensure that we expose our minds continually to God's Word? That we pray regularly and draw closer to God?

## II. Envy and Jealousy

1. What points did Paul make about envy and jealousy in:

   Romans 1:28-29?

   1 Corinthians 13:4?

Galatians 5:19-21?

2. Read these verses and make note of the kinds of things that tempt people to become envious and jealous:

Acts 5:12-17; 13:44-45:

1 Samuel 18:6-9:

Genesis 4:4-8; 37:4-11,18-20:

Esther 5:9-13:

3. Jerry writes, "Closely allied with envy and jealousy is the spirit of competitiveness — the urge to always win or be the top person in whatever our field of endeavor is." What's the difference between doing our best and being driven by envy and jealousy?

Doing Our Best: See 2 Timothy 2:15; Colossians 3:23; 1 Corinthians 9:24-27.

Being Driven by Envy or Jealousy: See Ecclesiastes 4:4; Song of Songs 8:6; James 3:16.

## TALK IT OVER
## FOR GROUP DISCUSSION

1. What kind of self-control, envy, and jealousy temptations do you face? What are some signals that we lack self-control, that our sinful desires are either starting to control us or have been controlling us?

2. What would you say are the three biggest areas in which people fail to exercise self-control? How can we recognize these temptations more quickly? What are the consequences? Practically speaking, how can we increase self-control when we are tempted to indulge our desires?

3. The author shares how a seemingly benign practice greatly weakened his self-control in more critical areas. In which areas are you tempted to use less self-control and give in to your desires?

4. Discuss this quote from chapter 18: "We cannot pick and choose the areas of life in which we will exercise self-control."

5. "Sinful jealousy occurs," writes the author, "when we are afraid someone is going to become equal to or even superior to us." Can you think of examples of this kind of jealousy? Why do you think it is displeasing to God?

6. If God is sovereign over the abilities and blessings He's given us, how should this truth influence our tendencies toward envy and sinful jealousy?

## GROUP PRAYER

Confess that you need God and His truth in order to vigilantly deal with "respectable" sins. Thank Him for His Holy Spirit, who lives within every believer and provides the power necessary to resist sin and draw closer to God. Pray for specific people in your group who have shared particular struggles. Close by affirming who God is and who He calls each believer to be.

❧ ❧

FOR NEXT TIME: Read *Respectable Sins*, chapters 20 and 21, and then respond to the "Think It Through" personal-study questions for session 9.

---

## TAKE IT TO HEART
*A PERSONAL-GROWTH JOURNAL*

### *Personal Reflection*

Reread the definition of self-control. Does lack of self-control keep surfacing in your life? If so, in which area(s)?

What role might the Holy Spirit play in helping you exercise more self-control?

Write out your response to this question: Is envy or sinful jealousy worth the energy? Explain your response.

If God were to underline any parts of this session with you in mind, what might He mark? Why?

### Personal Action Point

After rereading the definitions of self-control, envy, and jealousy, contemplate areas where they may have made inroads into your life. How do you plan to make progress over these "respectable" sins?

### Personal Prayer

Thank God for what you have learned during these sessions and ask for the will and power to keep dealing with "respectable" sins and pursuing the path He has for you.

---

BONUS ACTION POINTS

# Facing Up to Envy or Jealousy

When we are tempted to be envious or jealous, we can:

1. Remind ourselves of God's sovereignty. He gives us our talents, abilities, spiritual gifts, and opportunities (see 1 Samuel 2:7). To be envious or jealous of someone either eliminates God from the picture or accuses Him of being unfair.

2. Remember that all believers are "one body in Christ" and that each member of that body "belongs to all the others" (Romans 12:5, NIV). So, as Paul put it, "Outdo one another in showing honor" (Romans 12:10). Instead of being envious or jealous, let's honor and applaud people because we are all members of the same body in Christ. Let's submit to each other (see Ephesians 5:21).

3. Know that God has a place and assignment for each of us that He wants us to fill, and admittedly some of us garner more human recognition than others. If we spend emotional energy on envy or jealousy, we lose sight of what God might do uniquely in our lives. All assignments are important in God's plan.

# Good Jealousy?

Did you realize that not all jealousy is sinful? Being intolerant of rivalry can be godly. For example, if you are married and someone tries to win your spouse away from you, you feel legitimate jealousy. God, who declares Himself to be a jealous God, will not tolerate the worship of anyone or anything other than Him. Explore what the Bible says about God's jealousy:

Exodus 20:5:

Psalm 78:58:

Zechariah 1:14:

1 Corinthians 10:21-22:

## PROGRESS REPORT

Since the last session, have you discerned areas where you are lacking in self-control or are envious or jealous? How did you respond when these sins were brought to your attention?

As we talk about sins during this study, are you able to accept God's grace and forgiveness, along with His conviction, or do you find condemnation wanting to creep in?

How can we help each other become aware of and access God's grace in the face of our sin?

# Where Do We Go from Here?

BEFORE GATHERING: Read the following portion of *Respectable Sins*. In the margins, record observations, illustrations, or questions that come to mind as you read. Then answer the "Think It Through" study questions that follow the reading.

---

### Chapter Twenty: Worldliness

Worldliness means different things to different people. For our Amish friends, it means such things as electricity, telephones, and automobiles. For the very conservative church in which I grew up, it was a list of prohibited activities, such as dancing, card playing, and going to movies. Without meaning to denigrate either of these views, we should understand that worldliness is much broader than a list of prohibited activities or modern-day conveniences.

Two passages of Scripture will help us understand the concept of worldliness. The first is 1 John 2:15-16, where John exhorts us not to love the world and then describes the things of the world as the [sinful] desires of the flesh and the eyes as well as pride in possessions. These three expressions seem to indicate that John has in mind desires and attitudes that we would see today as being clearly sinful. Since, however, we have been considering what I call more acceptable or subtle sins, there is another passage from Paul that will help us understand the "acceptable" aspects of worldliness.

That passage is 1 Corinthians 7:31, which is translated in the New International Version as, ". . . those who use the things of the world, as if not engrossed in them. For this world in its present form is passing away." Different translations use different expressions to convey the same thought. The warning, then, is that though we use the legitimate things of the world, we should handle them with care lest they become too important to us.

Based on Paul's warning in 1 Corinthians 7:31, I define worldliness as *being attached to, engrossed in, or preoccupied with the things of this temporal life*. The things of this temporal life may or may not be sinful in themselves. What makes our attitude toward things that are not sinful worldliness is the high value we put upon them. Paul tells us in Colossians 3:2, "Set your minds on things that are above, not on things that are on earth." The things we value most should be "things that are above" — that is, spiritual things such as the Bible, prayer, the gospel, obedience to God, the fulfillment of the Great Commission, and most of all, God Himself. These are the areas where our values should be focused, not on even the legitimate things of this life.

The non-Christian world clearly does not focus on things of God. Even our nice, decent, but unbelieving neighbors are focused only on this life. By definition, they cannot be focused on the things that are above. Yet their lifestyles are outwardly not much, if any, different from ours. They mow their grass, pay their taxes, and avoid scandalous sins just like we do. That's why living among them makes worldliness look so acceptable to us. So we can further develop our understanding of worldliness by this secondary definition: Worldliness means accepting the values, mores, and practices of the nice, but unbelieving, society around us without discerning whether or not those values, mores, and practices are biblical. Worldliness is just going along with the culture around us as long as that culture is not obviously sinful.

Worldliness is a broad subject worthy of an entire book, and I'm devoting only a chapter to it. So I'm going to limit our discussion of it to three areas that I believe have become acceptable sins to us: money, immorality, and idolatry. This list may startle you because I have used two words — immorality and idolatry — that are clearly unacceptable. But there are certain aspects of both that have become acceptable, and it is those we will look at. And even with money, there are certain activities, such as stealing, fraud, and embezzlement, that are clearly unacceptable sins. So in all three areas, we will limit ourselves to what seems acceptable to us.

## MONEY

America is the wealthiest nation in the world, and our prosperous middle class is unparalleled in all of history. But the way we handle money is scandalous. In 2004, the average household income after taxes was $52,287. And yet, as I mentioned in session 8 (chapter 18), the average household credit card debt is $7,000. Even worse, from that income of over $52,000, the average household's giving for all causes was a mere $794 — about 1.5 percent.[1]

The above statistics are, of course, based on our entire population. Surely, evangelicals do better than that. Yes, they do, but not by much. In a 2003 survey, members of eight evangelical denominations gave 4.4 percent of their income to God's work. This was actually a decline from 6.2 percent that members of those same denominations gave in 1968.[2] If those eight denominations are reflective of evangelicalism as a whole, it means that we are becoming less generous toward God with our money.

Not only are we giving less to our churches, but it seems that more of what we do give is spent on ourselves. In 1920, the percentage of giving to missions from total offerings was just over 10 percent. But by 2003, that figure had declined to just under 3 percent. That means we spend 97 cents of every dollar on our own local programs and ministries while sending 3 cents overseas.[3]

So, in summary, it appears that evangelical households are keeping more of their income for themselves and giving less to their churches. And churches are keeping more of what they do receive for their own ministries and programs and sending less of it to missions working overseas. Yet we are the richest nation in history.

If our giving is decreasing and our credit card debt is increasing, what are we doing with our money? We know we are not saving it, for our savings, as a percentage of income, is also quite low — somewhere around 2 percent. What all this means is that we are spending it on the things of this life — houses, cars, clothes, vacations, and expensive electronic products, just to name a few. With our money we have set our minds not on the things above but on things that are on earth. We have become worldly in our use of money.

So how much should we be giving? I believe a minimum benchmark is 10 percent — or, to use a biblical expression, a tithe. I know there is some disagreement as to whether or not tithing is a biblical standard in our New Testament era since it is not mentioned specifically in any of the New Testament letters. But there is the concept of proportionate giving — that is, according as God has prospered us (see 1 Corinthians 16:2; 2 Corinthians 8:12). A tithe is a specific application of proportionate giving. Under it, the person who makes $10,000 gives $1,000. The person who makes $100,000 gives $10,000. Both people have given proportionally as God has prospered them. (There is the added thought that perhaps the person making $100,000 can afford to give more than 10 percent. That's why I regard the tithe as a minimum benchmark.)

I believe the concept of tithing has fallen on hard times, not because it is no longer considered a biblical concept but because we have become worldly in our attitude toward money and consequently have become stingy toward God. Stingy is a bad word. None of us would want to be accused of being stingy toward other people. We want to be known as generous folks. Yet when we voluntarily give less than half of what the Jews of the Old Testament were required to give, are we not being stingy? Is God pleased when we give less than half of what the Jews gave, especially when He described their failure to give their tithe as robbery of Him (see Malachi 3:8)?

Jesus said, "You cannot serve God and money" (Matthew

6:24). It appears that in the lives of many Christians, money is winning out over God. But God and money are not two equally good choices, because the Bible says, "For the love of money is a root of all kinds of evils. It is through this craving that some have wandered away from the faith and pierced themselves with many pangs" (I Timothy 6:10). If money wins out in our lives, it is not God but we who lose. Ultimately, God does not need our money. If we spend it on ourselves, it is we who become spiritual paupers.

Some Christians think they cannot afford to give 10 percent of their income to God's work. I understand that thinking. When I left industry to become a staff trainee with The Navigators years ago, I took a 75 percent cut in salary. I was financially shell-shocked. So I thought, "I can't afford to tithe. Surely, God accepts my sacrificial service at this low income as my giving." But God didn't let me get away with that for very long. So I decided I would tithe my meager income and trust God to provide.

A little later I was drawn to the story of Elijah being fed by the widow of Zarephath (see I Kings 17:8-16). She was down to her last bit of flour and oil with which she planned to prepare her last meal for her son and herself and then die. Yet Elijah said to her (and I'm paraphrasing), "Feed me first, for God will provide for you." She did as Elijah instructed her, and God did provide. The final sentence of the story says, "The jar of flour was not spent, neither did the jug of oil become empty, according to the word of the LORD that he spoke by Elijah" (verse 16). I began to pray over that verse, and I can tell you that throughout fifty-two years of ministry, God has always provided.

We need to remember that as we saw in session 3 (chapter 8), everything we have and the ability to earn more comes from God (I suggest you go back and reread Deuteronomy 8:17-18). Giving back to God at least 10 percent of what He has given us is a tangible expression of our recognition of that and our thanksgiving to Him for it. Finally, we need to remember the infinite generosity of our Lord in giving Himself for our salvation. When Paul wanted to encourage generosity among the Corinthians, he wrote, "You know the grace of our Lord Jesus Christ, that though he was rich, yet for your sake he became poor, so that you by his poverty might become rich" (2 Corinthians 8:9). Our giving should reflect the value we place on His gift to us.

## IMMORALITY

Of the three areas of worldliness we will look at, I'm sure this one raises the most eyebrows. You are no doubt wondering how immorality could ever be considered a respectable sin. Let me say right off that we are not going to address actual acts of immorality or adultery or even pornography. Those actions are clearly unacceptable and are beyond the scope of this book where we are looking at the sins we do tolerate.

So in what sense do we tolerate immorality? We do it by what a friend calls *vicarious immorality*. Do we secretly enjoy reading about the immorality of other people whose sexual misconduct is reported in our newspapers and weekly news magazines? If so, we are engaging in vicarious immorality. Do we sneak glances at the trashy tabloids and magazines on display at the supermarket checkout lines and secretly want to take one and read about the sexual exploits of the famous but openly immoral people? If so, we are engaging in vicarious immorality. If we go to movies or watch television programs knowing that sexually explicit sins will be shown or read novels knowing that such scenes will be described, we are engaging in vicarious immorality. It's clear that the world around us enjoys this sort of thing. After all, those tabloids and magazines wouldn't be at the checkout lane if our neighbors weren't buying them. And the same can be said of movies, TV programs, and novels. So this is one instance of values and practices accepted by society around us that are clearly contrary to Scripture. And to the extent that we follow along, we are worldly.

Then there is the area of immodest dress. As I walk along airport concourses or in shopping malls where large crowds of people are, I'm increasingly aware of the fashions women of all ages are wearing that are obviously intended to attract the lustful eyes of men. It seems that I'm constantly having to turn my eyes away from looking at something I should not see. And male students tell me that this problem is epidemic on their college campuses.

There are two areas under this subject in which we can become worldly. First, many Christian women, especially younger women, are going along with the styles of the unbelieving world around them. When my wife travels with me to visit university campuses, she is shocked and appalled by what some women students wear even to Christian meetings.

According to 1 Timothy 2:9, Christian women are to dress in respectable apparel with modesty and self-control. And so I say to the female readers of this book, if you simply go along with the immodest fashions of the day, you are worldly in this area of your life. And it's sad to say that this form of worldliness seems to be growing, especially among younger women.

For the men, our problem is responding to the immodest dress with lustful looks. It's not necessary for us to project that look into actual images of immorality. Even to linger with eyes and enjoy what women expose or accentuate by their tight garments is sin. We are simply doing what otherwise nice decent men around us are doing. And in that sense, we are worldly.

A younger man recently asked me how I handle this temptation. I told him my first line of defense is Proverbs 27:20, which I learned in the King James Version many years ago: "Hell and destruction are never full; so the eyes of man are never satisfied." The wording will be slightly different in any modern translation, but they all say the same thing. The application to me is that one lingering look never satisfies; it just whets the appetite for more. So don't linger over what you should not be looking at.

My second line of defense is Romans 6:21: "What fruit [that

is, benefit] were you getting at that time from the things of which you are now ashamed? The end of those things is death." I ask myself what benefit do I receive from indulging in a lustful look. And the answer is, Only the *fleeting* pleasures of sin, followed by thoughts of shame and regret. Men, let's commit ourselves to dealing with this area of worldliness.

## IDOLATRY

As we come to this section of worldliness, we again need some explanation. Obviously we are not worshiping idols of wood, metal, and stone these days. Our problem is what some call "idols of the heart." In this sense, an idol can be anything that we place such a high value on that it tends to absorb our emotional and mental energy, or our time and resources. Or it can be anything that takes precedence over our relationship with God or family.

A person's career or vocation can become an idol. The person becomes so obsessed with getting ahead or making it to the top that both God and family take second place. I recognize in the highly competitive world of business and industry, where so many of one's peers make their career their god, that it is difficult not to go along. Because the circumstances of each career or vocation are so different, there is no one-size-fits-all solution to the problem. There is, however, a biblical principle that, if kept in mind, will guard against the temptation to make an idol of one's career. That is the principle set forth by the apostle Paul in 2 Corinthians 5:9: "We make it our aim to please him." If your aim is to please God rather than climb the corporate ladder or be the most outstanding professional in your field, then you will avoid temptation to make an idol of your work.

I think of an automobile salesman I met some years ago. He said to me, "After I became a Christian, I stopped trying to *sell* cars and started helping people *buy* cars." He continued in the same vocation but with a different motive. His focus changed from how much money he would make to how he could serve people by helping them buy the car that would best fit their needs and their financial situation. He had changed his career from an idol to a service to God through genuinely serving people.

I realize that the application of Paul's principle may not be so clear in your situation. This is especially true in some careers where the corporate culture puts pressure on you for long hours and high productivity. If you find yourself in this situation, I urge you to get with a more mature Christian who can help you deal with the specific career issues you face.

A second possible area of idolatry is political and cultural issues. I combine these two because, in so many instances today, cultural issues have become political issues. While I believe it is important for Christians to be knowledgeable and, to some extent, involved in these issues, we have to be careful that we don't make idols of our political parties or our cultural concerns.

There is no question that there are cultural issues, such as abortion and homosexuality, that are clearly antithetical to God's moral standards. And I support those leaders and organizations that have committed themselves to stand against them. But we need to remember that the first priority of the church as a whole is the proclamation of the gospel. Unborn babies do need to be protected, and the biblical standard of marriage does need to be preserved. But above all, people need to be rescued from the power of Satan and brought into the kingdom of God through Jesus Christ. If we lose sight of the church's primary calling, then we are in danger of making an idol of our cultural and political initiatives.

A third area of modern-day idolatry is our consuming passion for sports. And here I know that, especially for many male readers, I'm walking into an area "where angels fear to tread." But I don't think there is any doubt that sports, especially football and basketball, have become idols in our culture. High school football is often spoken of as a religion in many states. Many high school coaches make large salaries. One at a suburban Alabama school makes $94,000 a year and puts his players through a training regimen almost as rigorous as that of professional athletes. In fact, this idolatry of sports no longer begins at the high school age. Now coaches are looking down into the elementary schools to find promising athletes whom they can begin to groom as high school players. And the ultra-competitive "winning is the only thing" attitude of many parents of these young players simply feeds this idolatry.

But it is really at the college level that idolatry is such a temptation. And I speak from experience. I'm a graduate of one of the schools whose football team has been a major powerhouse over the years. They have won seven national championships, the first of which occurred when I was a junior in college. I give you this background to explain why my school's football fortunes became something of an idol to me. Even years after I graduated, on Saturday game days I became as tense as if my happiness depended on the outcome of the day's game.

I'm not alone, and it is not just over football. Many fans of the perennial basketball powerhouses experience the same angst during basketball season and especially if their team makes it to the NCAA tournament. I'm still a fan of my university's football team, and I'm pleased when they win. But it's no longer an idol for me. God convicted me of my idolatry, and I now remind myself that football is only a game, and I don't think God is glorified regardless of who wins. The truth is that winning only panders to our pride.

So continue to root for your favorite team, if you desire. But don't get caught up in its wins and losses. Keep sports in perspective. It's only a game.

Now let me review my twofold definition of worldliness. First of all, it's a preoccupation with the things of this temporal life. Second, it's accepting and going along with the values and practices of society around us without discerning if they are biblical. I believe the key to our tendencies toward worldliness lies primarily in the two words *going along*. We simply go along

214

with and accept the values and practices of society around us without thought as to whether those values and practices are biblical. That's why Christian young women will wear immodest dress. They simply go along with the styles others are wearing without stopping to think whether or not those styles are pleasing to God. And there is nothing overtly sinful in sports themselves. But if we simply go along with others around us, we can end up making an idol of our favorite team.

How, then, can we deal with our tendencies toward worldliness? It is not by determining that we will not be worldly but by committing ourselves to becoming more godly. We need to grow in our relationship with Him and begin to view all aspects of life through the lens of His glory. In the nineteenth century, a Scottish minister, Thomas Chalmers, preached a sermon called "The Expulsive Power of a New Affection." That's what we need to combat our worldliness. We need an increased affection for God that will expel from our hearts our affections for the things of this world.

## Chapter Twenty-One:
## Where Do We Go from Here?

If you have stayed with me this far, you know that we have worked through some pretty bad stuff. We have looked in detail at many of the subtle sins we tolerate in our lives. At times, this may have been painful. I hope it has, because that means you have been honest enough and humble enough to admit the presence of some of these sins in your own life. And in this, there is hope. Remember, "God opposes the proud but gives grace to the humble" (1 Peter 5:5).

The opening statements of the Sermon on the Mount (see Matthew 5:1-7) should encourage you. The poor in spirit and those who mourn are those who are conscious of their own sinfulness. Because of this, they are meek and merciful in their attitudes and actions toward others, and they hunger and thirst for the righteousness that they realize they have not yet attained. Their whole demeanor is exactly opposite that of the proud, morally superior, self-righteous person. Yet Jesus said that they (not the self-righteous people) are the ones who are blessed.

In telling His parables, Jesus created the characters to make His points in a most forceful way. Consider the parable of the Pharisee and the tax collector praying in the temple (see Luke 18:9-14). In the eyes of the Jews, the contrast between a Pharisee and a hated tax collector could not have been greater. And in the parable of the prodigal son (see Luke 15:11-32), the son's despicable actions would have scandalized His Jewish audience. Yet in the two parables, it is the self-righteous Pharisee and the self-righteous older brother who receive the implied condemnation of Jesus. Meanwhile, the tax collector goes away justified, and the repentant prodigal son is received into the warm embrace of his father. Does this not tell us something about how much God hates the sin of self-righteousness and how He responds graciously to a humble and contrite spirit?

I concluded the last chapter with a reference to Thomas Chalmers' sermon "The Expulsive Power of a New Affection." The question naturally arises, "How can we grow in this new affection?" The answer is that it comes from an increasing awareness of our still-remaining sinfulness and of Christ's love for us in dying for that sin.

In Luke's account of the sinful woman who washed and anointed the feet of Jesus (7:36-50), Jesus said, "He who is forgiven little, loves little" (verse 47). The opposite is also true, as Jesus clearly indicates in verses 41-43; that is, he who is forgiven much, loves much. Simon the Pharisee did not realize how sinful he was and how much he needed to be forgiven, so he loved little or actually not at all. The sinful woman realized how sinful she was and how much she had been forgiven, so she loved much. The way to grow in our new affection [for Christ] that Chalmers preached about is to grow in our awareness of Christ's love for us as revealed to us in the gospel. The apostle Paul wrote that it is Christ's love *for us* that constrains us to live for Him (see 2 Corinthians 5:14-15). Such love for Him that will drive out our love for the world can only be a response to the deep, heartfelt sense of His love for us.

So we need to be honest and humble enough to admit our subtle sins in order to experience the love that comes through the forgiveness of those sins. But we must also face them in order to deal with them. The worst sin of all, in practical terms, is the denial of the subtle sins in our lives. We cannot deal with them until we admit their presence. The first step in dealing with any sin is to acknowledge it and repent in one's attitude toward it. This doesn't mean we will make rapid progress in getting those sins out of our lives. The flesh doesn't give up that easily. Rather, to use Paul's term, these subtle sins must be "put to death" (Romans 8:13; Colossians 3:5). Furthermore, we have developed habits of sinning. We have developed habits of ungodly thinking: anxiety, self-indulgence, critical attitudes, gossip, and the like. So where do we go from here? How can we apply the overall message of this book?

I hope as we've been going along over these so-called "respectable" sins that you have honestly prayed over each one, asking God to reveal to you any evidence of them in your life. But, at this time, it would be good to take a prayerful review. To facilitate this, here is a skeletal outline of the subtle sins we have discussed:

Chapter 7 — Ungodliness
Chapter 8 — Unthankfulness
  • Thankfulness in difficult circumstances
Chapter 9 — Anxiety and Frustration
Chapter 10 — Discontentment
Chapter 11 — Pride
  • Moral self-righteousness

Notes and Observations

- Pride of correct doctrine
- Pride of achievement
- An independent spirit

Chapter 12 — Selfishness
- Our interests
- Our time
- Our money
- Inconsiderateness

Chapter 13 — Impatience and Irritability

Chapter 14 — Anger
- Anger toward God

Chapter 15 — The Weeds of Anger
- Resentment
- Bitterness
- Enmity and hostility
- Grudges

Chapter 16 — Judgmentalism
- Over differing convictions
- Over doctrinal disagreement
- A critical spirit

Chapter 17 — Sins of the Tongue
- Gossip
- Slander
- Lying
- Harsh words, sarcasm, insults, and ridicule

Chapter 18 — Lack of Self-Control
- Eating and drinking
- With one's temper
- Personal finances
- Television, hobbies, impulse buying

Chapter 19 — Envy, Jealousy, and Related Sins
- Envy
- Jealousy
- Competitiveness
- Controlling

Chapter 20 — Worldliness

- Money
- Vicarious immorality
- Idolatry

As you go over this list, continue to ask God to open your eyes to sins you have been tolerating or have even refused to acknowledge as being present in your life. There is no substitute for humility and honest confession of our sin as the first step in dealing with it.

Have you asked others for their evaluation of the presence of these subtle sins in your life? If not, this would be a good time to do it. Set aside time with your spouse, your brother or sister, or a good friend. Ask for their honest feedback. Assure them you will not become defensive or question their evaluation. Just listen but don't respond. You might ask them to rate you in each area according to a scale something like this:

- Not a problem
- Occasionally a problem
- Frequently a problem
- Characteristic of your life

Even if you don't agree with their assessments, take them to heart in humility. God may be using the other person to open up areas you have been in denial about.

Go back and review the six directions for dealing with sin set forth in session 2 (chapter 6). And if you are overwhelmed at this time, pay special attention to the first direction to always address your sin in the context of the gospel.

Remember that our progressive sanctification — that is, our putting off sin and putting on Christlikeness — rests on two foundation stones: the righteousness of Christ and the power of the Holy Spirit. Always look to Christ and His perfect righteousness for your standing and your acceptableness to God. Remember, if you are united to Christ, God sees you clothed in His perfect righteousness. And always look to the Holy Spirit

Notes and Observations

to enable you to deal with sin in your life and to produce in you the fruit of the Spirit.

The world around us watches us even as it ridicules our values and rejects our message. We may think our subtle sins are hidden from their view, but in some way they see them. They pick up our self-righteousness, our anger, and our judgmentalism. They think of us as "holier-than-thou" people or else they see us as hypocrites who do not practice what we preach. Dealing with our "acceptable" sins in humility and honesty can go a long way in dispelling that image. Finally, let me repeat the words of 1 Peter 5:5: "God opposes the proud but gives grace to the humble."

# Where Do We Go from Here?

## (Chapters 20 and 21)

## STUDY QUESTIONS

KEY VERSES: "Set your minds on things that are above, not on things that are on earth. . . . Blessed are those who hunger and thirst for righteousness, for they shall be satisfied. . . . God opposes the proud but gives grace to the humble." (Colossians 3:2; Matthew 5:6; 1 Peter 5:5)

### GET FOCUSED

Many of us think of a list of prohibited activities when we hear the word *worldliness*. Yet Jerry Bridges is speaking of the tendency to become preoccupied with things of the world or to go along unthinkingly with the culture around us — particularly in the areas of money, immorality, and idolatry. The thought of those three areas involving subtle sins may startle us. Immorality and idolatry aren't subtle at all! However, there are aspects of all three areas where we have lost sensitivity and discernment. We simply accept the values and practices of society without thought as to whether those values and practices are biblical.

The antidote for worldliness isn't to come up with a list of prohibited activities or associates. Rather, it is a determination to become more godly, a process that begins as we grow in relationship with God and affection for Him.

In fact, a growing affection for God is the antidote to all of our subtle sins. That growth comes from an increasing awareness of our still-remaining sinfulness and of Christ's love for us in dying for that sin. While looking at our sins can be painful, there is hope: "God opposes the proud but gives grace to the humble" (1 Peter 5:5). When we are honest and humble enough to admit our subtle sins, we experience the love that comes through forgiveness.

## THINK IT THROUGH
### FOR PERSONAL STUDY

### *I. Worldliness*

1. Read the following passages. How does letting our hearts be drawn toward the world affect our love for God?

James 4:4-5:

1 John 2:15:

2. Both passages use strong words to describe how affection for the world changes our relationship with God. Why is it so hard to enter into friendship with both God *and* the world? (See John 17:13-16 and 1 Peter 2:9-10.)

3. Jerry talked about the truth embedded in a sermon by Thomas Chalmers, "The Expulsive Power of a New Affection." Here is what Chalmers said about displacing our love for the world:

"There are two ways in which a practical moralist may attempt to displace from the human heart its love of the world — either by a demonstration of the world's vanity, so as that the heart shall be prevailed upon simply to withdraw its regards from an object that is not worthy of it; or, by setting forth another object, even God, as more worthy of its attachment, so as that the heart shall be prevailed upon . . . to exchange an old affection for a new one."

—THOMAS CHALMERS[4]

What two methods does Chalmers identify as ways of detaching our hearts from love of the world?

a.

b.

4. Have you tried either or both of these methods? Describe your experience(s).

   a. Convincing my heart not to love something unworthy: _____

   b. Finding something more worthy to love: _____

5. How does a new affection disrupt your tendency to go along with the status quo? (If you need an example, think of a time you fell in love with something or someone and how that new focus changed your routine ways of thinking and acting.)

## *II. Where Do We Go from Here?*

1. Throughout *Respectable Sins,* Jerry has been helping us see areas in which we may have been coasting along, not noticing our sins because they seem so acceptable. How has this study altered your attitude toward sin?


2. Read the following verses and note the attitudes or actions that will help us as we consider our sins, along with the outcomes or promises given to those who hold the attitudes.

| ATTITUDES OR ACTIONS | PROMISES OR OUTCOMES |
| --- | --- |

Matthew 5:3:


Matthew 5:5:


Matthew 5:6:


James 4:4-10:


3. Where would you like God to give you continued help and empowering as you struggle with sin?


4. As we saw above, "the expulsive power of a new affection" is a tremendous aid in moving us away from sin and toward the life we want with God. Write a prayer to God, asking Him for that aid. Ask Him to give you such a taste of His care and love for you that you are moved toward humility, meekness, and affection in response.

## TALK IT OVER
### FOR GROUP DISCUSSION

1. In session 1, the first question in the "Think It Through" section asked, "Why do you think it's important for us to understand what sin is and its impact on our lives and relationships?" How would you answer that question now, at the end of the study?

2. How has this study affected your view of Jesus' sacrifice for you on the cross?

3. Read Luke 7:36-50 together. If you had been sitting next to Jesus at that table, what might your response have been? For example, would you have identified with the woman who was so expressively grateful to Jesus? Might you have found it easier to understand Simon — or had a different response entirely?

4. Notice how this passage focuses on relationship. The sinful woman demonstrates intense love for Jesus. And Jesus asks Simon which forgiven debtor will *love* the money-lender more — not which debtor will be happier or more likely to forgive another's debt. How would you explain this interplay between sin, forgiveness, and loving God?

5. Over the past weeks, what has God revealed personally to you about His heart toward you and His willingness to forgive you and make you clean? How has that altered your affection for Him?

6. How would you like this study to continue to affect you in the weeks ahead?

## GROUP PRAYER

Thank God for His grace, for His generous forgiveness because of the sacrifice of Jesus, and for His ongoing empowering through the Holy Spirit. Pray for each other, that in the weeks to come you will experience a deeper awareness of sin and forgiveness that will lead you to love God more.

# Help for Group Leaders

The following pages are designed to help a discussion leader guide a group through this study. You can appoint one person to lead each session, or you can rotate leadership.

## GETTING STARTED

Choose a time and place to meet that is consistent, comfortable, and relatively free from distractions. If you meet in a home, make plans to deal with pets, ringing telephones, and other distractions.

### SET YOUR SESSION FORMAT.

Decide how long your sessions will be, and map out a general plan for each gathering. Following is a sample format for a sixty-minute session.

- *Ten minutes* for settling in, opening prayer, and warm-up conversation. Refreshments can help people mingle, but don't let them consume too much of your time.
- *Forty minutes* for discussion of the study questions. Open your discussion by inviting group members to share their responses to the chapter(s) they read during the week. Then move into discussing the questions that followed the session's reading.
- *Ten minutes* for closing prayer time and closing comments. Before you end, call attention to the next session's readings and encourage group members to complete the study questions on their own.

### CUSTOMIZE THE MATERIAL FOR YOUR GROUP.

As you facilitate each group session, you'll move through the following elements in the study guide.

- *Text.* Each session opens with the chapters in *Respectable Sins* to be read before gathering. You'll want to call attention to the next session's assigned readings at the close of each meeting. Participants are also encouraged to work through the corresponding "Think It Through" study questions prior to each group session.

- *Progress Report.* At the end of each session you'll find a "Progress Report" — a quick personal-application review of some of the key principles. Start each group experience by posing these questions from the previous session and encouraging participants to share their personal discoveries and/or spiritual progress. You'll all be encouraged as you hear what your friends are learning!

- *Key Verse(s) and Get Focused.* After the progress report, have everyone follow along as one group member reads aloud the "Key Verse(s)" and the "Get Focused" section. This underscores the importance of the chapters they've read during the week and sets the tone for the coming discussion.

- *Think It Through.* Take a few minutes to ask for questions or insights participants may have gained in their study of the "Think It Through" section during the week. (Tip: Preselect a couple of the questions and insights to highlight in case people did not complete this section.)

- *Talk It Over.* Devote the bulk of the discussion time to the "Talk It Over" questions designed for group discussion.

- *Group Prayer.* Conclude by praying together. We've provided suggested topics under "Group Prayer" to get the prayer time started.

- *For Next Time.* Take a moment to point out the "For Next Time" assignments for the next session. For the best learning experience, we encourage participants to make quality time to read the assigned chapters and respond to the corresponding "Think It Through" study questions. However, you may want to assure them that if they can read only the assigned book chapters, that's fine — they can dig in to the "Think It Through" section some other time.

- *Take It to Heart.* Encourage participants to take the time to enjoy the personal journaling experience provided at the end of each session. Responding to the guided prompts in these "Take It to Heart" segments will enhance their personal understanding and life application of the principles you've discussed.

Leaders should decide which questions and elements to cover during group time. You probably will not have time to discuss all questions in depth; focus on the ones that are most important for your group. When a question is about a Scripture passage, it will be helpful to read the passage together. When there are a number of passages, decide which ones to discuss during group time.

Please note that the number of sessions in the study guide doesn't correlate directly with the numbers of chapters in the book. This resource combines two or three book chapters into each session. We created it this way to compress the sessions into a shorter amount of time (nine weeks, if you do one session per week) than the book would allow (twenty-one chapters). If you want to create a longer study, you might cover some sessions in two weeks instead of one.

## Plan your first session.

You may want to plan a potluck for your first meeting together. In this way, group members can get to know one another in the context of a meal, which is a good way to break down barriers. Then after dinner you can have your first session.

The content you cover in this session depends on which of the following options you choose.

*Option one: A nine-week study.* This is how we've set up this book. In this format, make sure each participant has a copy of this book prior to session 1. Encourage everyone to read the chapters and respond to the study questions for session 1 prior to your first meeting.

*Option two: A ten-week study.* In this option, you add an additional "opening week" to use for distributing the books and getting acquainted with group members. In this session, have someone read aloud "A Note from the Author" on page 7 as the group follows along. Encourage participants to talk about their responses to what Jerry Bridges is saying. Talk together about group members' expectations for the study. Are they anticipating the topic or does the idea of talking about sins make them nervous? Pray together for open hearts and minds; for an awareness that God is present, engaged, and interested in your discussions; and for a spirit of mutual encouragement as you study and discuss the book during the coming weeks. Then assign the preparation under option one above for your next meeting — the real "session 1" of this study.

Whichever option you choose, be sure to set aside adequate time in the first meeting for people to share who they are. It is amazing how much more productive and honest a

Bible discussion is when the participants know each other.

At some point in the evening (probably toward the end), go over the following guidelines. They help make a discussion more fruitful, especially when you are dealing with issues that truly matter to people.

- *Trustworthiness and respect.* No one should repeat what someone shares in the group unless that person gives express permission. Even then, discretion is imperative. Be trustworthy. Participants should talk about their own feelings and experiences, not those of others.
- *Attendance.* Each session builds on the previous ones, and you need each other. So, ask group members to commit to attending all sessions, unless an emergency arises.
- *Participation.* This is a group discussion, not a lecture. It is important that each person participate in some way.
- *Preparation.* Encourage everyone to read the material and answer the questions before the group meets. Your discussions will be more interesting if group members have prepared in advance. In addition, group members will get far more out of the study if they have spent time thinking about the questions and meditating on the Scriptures before meeting.
- *Honesty.* Appropriate openness is a key to a good group. Be who you really are, not who you think you ought to be.
- *Transformation.* The goal of this study is to come to know God's heart and character in a way that leads to transformation from the inside out. As you read and study, please allow God to take you past simply gaining knowledge to encountering Him in fresh ways.

## GENERAL HELPS

Below, we have provided general helps for leading your group, but we can't cover every situation you will encounter — such as a group that talks too much or a group that won't discuss at all. Talk with veteran leaders in your church when you need input and ideas. And remember: Your greatest help is always God's Holy Spirit, who has committed to living with you and doing life with you. He's an extraordinary teacher, and you can rely on His strength, wisdom, and problem-solving skills for your group.

## Preparing for a Session

Your aim as a leader is to prepare an environment that is conducive to growth. You want group members to feel comfortable with one another so they freely engage with the material and discussion.

*Pray for the group.* As the group leader, your most important preparation for each session is prayer. You will want to make your prayers personal, of course, but here are some suggestions for how to pray:

- Let God be the leader of the group. Ask Him to show you what portions and questions to emphasize and how to format the discussion. Invite God to give you input on your group's unique needs each week.
- Ask the Holy Spirit to bring alive the truths you are studying, personalizing them for each group member.
- Pray that nothing will keep the group members from attending. Ask God to enable them to feel free to share their thoughts and feelings honestly and to contribute their unique gifts and insights.
- Pray for group members' private times with God this week. Ask God to be active in nurturing them.
- Ask for the Holy Spirit's guidance in exercising patience, acceptance, sensitivity, and wisdom as you talk with each other. Pray for an atmosphere of genuine love in the group, with each member being open to learning and change.
- Pray that your discussion will lead each of you to love the Lord more deeply, obey Him more closely, and demonstrate His presence more tangibly.
- Pray for insight as you go over the study materials and for wisdom as you lead the group so that you tap into God's desires for your time together.

*Study and customize the material.* After prayer, your most important preparation is to be thoroughly familiar with the material you will discuss. You will find it important to read the chapters that are covered by each session and to make sure you have answered all of the questions.

Decide which questions you want to discuss as a group. You may not have time to cover all the questions. Consider and ask God about which questions are most important for your particular group.

## LEADING A SESSION

Following are general guidelines for leading a group discussion. If you are a new leader, you can also ask an experienced group leader to mentor you.

*Invite God to be the leader.* Open each session with prayer, acknowledging that God is present with the group and that He has an "agenda" for the session. Surrender your plan for the time to Him and invite Him to work in and speak to group members.

*Work toward a relaxed and open atmosphere.* This may not come quickly, so be a model for the others of acceptance, openness to truth and change, and love. Develop a genuine interest in each person's remarks and expect to learn from them. Show that you care by listening carefully. Be affirming.

*Invite opening comments.* Open your discussion by inviting group members to share any responses, observations, or questions about the chapter(s) they read. If a group member brings up a point that will be discussed later in the session, affirm what a good point it is and mention that you'll be talking more about this later. This will help keep your discussion from getting sidetracked at the beginning.

*Pay attention to how you ask the questions.* Don't ask flatly, "What did you get for number 1?" Instead, by your tone of voice convey your interest and enthusiasm for the question and your warmth toward the group. The group will adopt your attitude. Read the questions as though you were asking them of good friends.

*Vary your approach as you move through the questions.* For some questions you might pose the issue to no one in particular and wait for responses. For others, you might direct the question to a specific individual, let him or her respond, and then encourage others to respond as well. As much as time permits, encourage unrushed multiple responses. Sometimes you'll discover deeper levels of insight as one participant builds upon the thoughts of another.

*Expect variations or pauses in the discussion.* Sometimes a group won't respond as quickly as you'd like. If that happens . . .

- Be comfortable with silence. Let the group wrestle to think of answers. Don't be quick to jump in and rescue the group with your answers.
- Reword a question if the group members have trouble understanding it.
- If a question evokes little response, feel free to leave it and move on.
- Feel free to answer questions yourself occasionally. In particular, you might need to be the first one to answer questions about personal experiences. In

this way you will model the depth of openness and thought you hope others will show. You can also model an appropriate length of response. Don't answer every question, but don't be a silent observer.

- If the discussion is winding down on a question, go on to the next one. It's not necessary to push people to see every possible angle.

*Ask only one question at a time.* Often, participants' responses will suggest a follow-up question to you. Be discerning as to when you are following a fruitful train of thought and when you are going off on a tangent.

*Be aware of time.* Don't spend so much time discussing that you run out of time for application and prayer. Your goal is not to have something to discuss but to become more like Jesus Christ.

*Encourage constructive controversy.* The group can learn a lot from struggling with the many sides of an issue. If you aren't threatened when someone disagrees, the whole group will be more open and vulnerable. Intervene, if necessary, to be sure that people are debating ideas and interpretations of Scripture, not attacking each other's feelings and character. If the group gets stuck in an irresolvable argument, say something such as, "We can agree to disagree here," and move on.

*Don't be the expert.* People will stop talking if they feel you are judging their answers or that you think you know best. Let God's words in the Bible be the expert, the final say. Let people candidly express their feelings and experiences.

*Don't do for the group what it can do for itself.* With a beginning group, you may have to ask all of the questions, do all of the outside research, plan the applications, etc. But within a few meetings you should start delegating various leadership responsibilities. Let members learn to exercise their gifts. Let them start making decisions and solving problems together. Encourage them to maturity and unity in Christ.

*Encourage people to share feelings as well as facts.* There are two dimensions of truth: the truth about how people feel, and the truth about who God is. People need to face both their real feelings and the real God.

*Summarize the discussion frequently.* Help the group see where the discussion is going.

*Let the group plan applications.* The action responses in this guide are suggestions. Your group should adapt them so they are relevant and life-changing for members. If group members aren't committed to an application, they won't do it. Encourage, but don't force.

*Allow freedom during your prayer times.* To close a meeting, you can have one person pray or open up the time for brief conversational prayers from anyone who wishes to pray aloud. (Tip: No one should ever feel pressured or obligated to pray aloud. It can help everyone relax if you assure them of this ahead of time.) You might use your prayer time to pray for group members' general needs, or suggest that you pray personally for each member regarding the insights and struggles he or she encountered with this session. Feel free to allow silence during prayer so that God has space to respond individually to group members' prayers.

## REVIEWING AFTER A SESSION

Use the following questions each week to help you improve your leadership next time.

1. How did you see God at work during your time together?
2. Did you have the right number of questions prepared? Should you add to the next session's questions or plan to cover fewer questions?
3. Did you discuss the major issues? If you missed major points, on your notes for next week mark the essential questions or points you want to cover and summarize.
4. Did you know your material thoroughly enough to have freedom in leading?
5. Did you keep the discussion from wandering?
6. Did everyone participate? Were people open? Was anyone overtalkative? Disruptive? Think about how you can handle these problems next week if they occur again, or ask another group leader for ideas.
7. Was the discussion practical? Did it lead to new understanding, new hope, repentance, change? If necessary, brainstorm some application questions that can help lead the group in this direction.
8. Did you begin and end on time? If necessary, put a clock or watch in plain sight in your meeting area so you can easily glance at it and keep track of time.
9. Did you give the group the maximum responsibility that it can handle?
10. What does God think of the time together?
11. How would He want to be your coach and mentor as you lead next week? If you're feeling inadequate in some area of leadership, how would He want to be strong for you and provide the power, wisdom, and expertise you need?
12. How does He want to affirm you for your investment in leading this group? Where is He proud of you and pleased with you, as a proud Father might be?

# Notes

### Session One: Facing Up to the Truth

1. Karl Menninger, MD, *Whatever Became of Sin?* (New York: Hawthorne Books, 1973), 14–15.
2. Peter Barnes, "What! Me? A Sinner?" *The Banner of Truth*, April 2004, 21.
3. Marsha Witten, *All Is Forgiven* (Princeton, NJ: Princeton University Press, 1993), 81.
4. Witten, 101–102.
5. Ralph Venning, *The Sinfulness of Sin* (Edinburgh, Scotland, and Carlisle, PA: The Banner of Truth Trust, 1965, first published 1669), 31.
6. Menninger, 14–15.

### Session Two: The Remedy for Sin

1. Brian H. Edwards, *Through Many Dangers: The Story of John Newton* (Welwyn, England: Eurobooks, 1980), 191.
2. An alternate reading of the last phrase is "Save from wrath and make me pure." Of ten hymnals I consulted, five use the phrase I have used. Five use the alternate reading. Either way, the meaning is ultimately the same.
3. An exposition and application to life of some of these Scriptures is included in chapter 6 of my book *The Gospel for Everyday Life*, also published by NavPress.
4. Edwards, 191.

### Session Four: Anxiety, Frustration, and Discontentment

1. John Newton, *Letters of John Newton* (Carlisle, PA: The Banner of Truth Trust, 1960), 137.
2. I am aware that some people suffer from extreme anxiety attacks that are totally consuming and often result in physical complications. These cases may require professional help and are beyond the scope of this book. I am dealing with what we might call the anxieties of ordinary, daily life.
3. From "In Acceptance Lieth Peace," page 293 of *Mountain Breezes* by Amy

Carmichael. Copyright 1999 by Dohnavur Fellowship, and published by CLC Publications, Fort Washington, PA. All rights reserved. Used by permission.

4. I have dealt with these attributes of God more in depth in my book *Trusting God: Even When Life Hurts* (NavPress).

5. Newton, 137.

## SESSION SIX: **Impatience, Irritability, and Anger**

1. This expression is taken from the title of the book, *War of Words* by Paul David Tripp, P&R Publishing, Phillipsburg, NJ. This is an excellent book that I highly recommend.

2. Robert D. Jones, *Uprooting Anger* (Phillipsburg, NJ: P & R Publishing, 2005), 13.

3. I am indebted to Robert Jones for these thoughts, though I have not quoted him exactly. For readers who want to pursue the subject of anger beyond this chapter, Jones' book *Uprooting Anger* is an excellent resource.

4. I realize that the scriptural principles for marriage taught by Paul and Peter in Ephesians 5:22-33 and 1 Peter 3:1-7 should govern these situations, but I am dealing with the anger that results when they are not observed.

5. Again I know that I have treated this subject lightly. Robert Jones has an excellent chapter in his book (cited previously) that deals extensively with the subject of anger against God.

6. Some readers may wonder why I do not refer to the phrase "root of bitterness" in Hebrews 12:15 as a warning against the sin of bitterness. The expression is an allusion to Deuteronomy 29:18 and the phrase "poisonous and bitter fruit," which in that passage speaks of inward, heart rebellion against God. In Hebrews 12:15, the writer is using that expression from Deuteronomy to warn against apostasy, not the bitterness of ongoing resentment.

## SESSION NINE: **Where Do We Go from Here?**

1. Joel Belz, "Stingy Givers," *World Magazine*, June 24, 2006, 4.

2. Belz, 4.

3. Gene Edward Veith, "Who Gives Two Cents for Missions?" *World Magazine*, October 22, 2005, 28.

# About the Author

Jerry Bridges is an author and Bible teacher. His most popular book, *The Pursuit of Holiness*, has sold over one million copies. He is also the author of *Trusting God*, *The Discipline of Grace*, *The Practice of Godliness*, *The Fruitful Life*, and *The Gospel for Real Life*. As a full-time staff member with The Navigators for many years, Jerry has served in the collegiate ministry and community ministries.